Costa Rica

A Kick Start Guide for Business Travelers

Costa Rica

A Kick Start Guide for Business Travelers

Guy & Victoria Brooks

Self-Counsel Press
(*a division of*)
International Self-Counsel Press Ltd.
Canada U.S.A.

Printed in Canada

First edition: May, 1996

Canadian Cataloguing in Publication Data
Brooks, Guy, 1955-
Costa Rica

(Self-counsel series)
ISBN 1-55180-025-X

1. Business travel — Costa Rica. 2. Costa Rica — Economic conditions — 1948- 3. Costa Rica — Guidebooks. I. Brooks, Victoria, 1951- II. Title. III. Series.
F1543.5.B76 1996 917.28604'5 C96-910146-5

Self-Counsel Press
(a division of)
International Self-Counsel Press Ltd.

1481 Charlotte Road
North Vancouver, B.C.
V7J 1H1

1704 N. State Street
Bellingham, Washington
98225

For Tyson, our bright and shining light who gets better every year and without whose help, love, unflagging interest, and support for us none of this would be possible.

Notice to Readers

Every effort is made to keep this publication as current as possible. However, it is the nature of travel books that some information could become outdated between the time of writing and publication. Prices, telephone and fax numbers, addresses, and hours of operation of businesses are subject to change without notice. Readers are asked to take this into account when consulting this guide. If you would like to contact the authors, they can be reached at their e-mail address: kikstart@axionet.com.

The authors, the publisher, and the vendor of this book make no representation or warranties regarding the outcome or the use to which the information in this book is put, and are not assuming any liability for any claims, losses, or damages arising out of the use of this book. The reader should not rely on the author or the publisher of this book for any professional advice.

Contents

Maps

Acknowledgments

Information about Costa Rica is infamous for being confusing or incomplete. Thank you to all these people and others too numerous to mention for giving us their valuable time and sharing their knowledge with us to make this guide as comprehensive as possible.

Special thanks to Tyson Brooks, as always, for his valuable contribution to the research and writing; to Fred Kerner in Toronto for his knowledge and unstinting generosity; also to the Instituto Costarricense de Turismo, without whose help we could not have written this guide; and to our skilled and kind driver Gerrardo. Thanks to American Airlines in Fort Worth, Texas; Lynda Solar of the American Chamber of Commerce in Costa Rica; the Canadian consulate in San José; the Costa Rican Coalition for Development Initiatives in San José; Carlos Arrea and associates at KPMG-Peat Marwick in San José; Jerry Smith, president of Tamarindo Real Estate in Santa Cruz, Guanacaste; Lic. Ronald Blair Houston M., attorney at law in San José; Erik Steinberg of PropData in San José; and Esteban Diaz J., Panama's consul general in Vancouver, British Columbia.

MEXICO
CUBA
JAMAICA
BELIZE
GUATEMALA
HONDURAS
EL SALVADOR
NICARAGUA
COSTA RICA
Liberia
Puntarenas
San Jose
Bocas del Toro
Golfito
PANAMA
COLUMBIA

Introduction

Who Should Read *Costa Rica*

This guide was specifically researched and written for the business traveler who is on the lookout for new opportunities in Costa Rica, a country trying to live up to its name, which in English means "rich coast."

Costa Rica has been depicted as a nearly perfect tropical land and as an entrepreneur's dream — the California of the 1990s. It has beckoned anyone wanting to set up and run a small business in a warm climate. It tempts those who think of dabbling in coffee, orange, or teak plantations. New opportunities are blossoming in infrastructure, agriculture, exports, tourism, real estate, and in consumer, corporate, and financial services.

Bananas and coffee continue to be Costa Rica's largest exports. Other traditional exports are sugar, beef products, and chocolate. But nontraditional exports are where the profit is; lucrative new crops like mangoes, papayas, and pineapples are exported for use in baby food, jams, and health food products. Other nontraditional exports include preprinted packages for juices, foods, and other goods; ornamental plants; fertilizer; and medicine.

In 1990, Costa Rica began the move to become an open market; General Agreement on Tariffs and Trade (GATT) accords were signed and tariffs were dropped. Free trade zones opened in which entrepreneurs set up factories to assemble industrial exports like textiles and electrical equipment.

In the mid 1990s, the tourism industry became Costa Rica's biggest earner of foreign currency with an annual intake of over US $600 million. Supplying services and products for foreign tourists can be good business.

Tip: There is a big demand for souvenirs of Costa Rica, but few producers have stepped in to fill this market. The entrepreneur with imagination and energy can set up rain forest, volcano, and wildlife tours; hot springs resorts; butterfly farms; and other nature attractions inland, away from the country's beaches.

The best opportunities will appear in the coming years. Costa Rica is attracting overseas investment by privatizing industries traditionally run by the government. Recent and ongoing changes include the privatization of banking and public works (such as cement production and the

National Liquor Factory), creating opportunities in finance, infrastructure, and construction. To top that, Costa Rica's real estate boom has peaked and prices are on the way down, making this the best time for the patient entrepreneur to acquire real estate.

Doing business in Costa Rica can be rewarding but, as with any venture, the risks are great and the entrepreneur must play by the Costa Rican rules. The key to business success is to step carefully with your eyes wide open. If you come armed with the knowledge of how to do business and know what to watch out for, the payoff can be well worth the effort.

How to Use *Costa Rica*

Our task in writing this guide is to show you, the business traveler, where to start the research and groundwork necessary to do business in Costa Rica, while avoiding common but unfamiliar pitfalls. The result will be an easier adjustment for you, which means your mind can focus on recognizing and implementing opportunities instead of dealing with culture shock.

We had heard from business travelers to Costa Rica that any sort of information, from concrete statistics to contact names or the names of departments to access for help in achieving business goals, is notoriously hard to get in any sector. Data is either skimpy, contradictory, or totally nonexistent. We have done our best to help you find information, identify opportunities, and, most important, sort the dream from the reality.

Costa Rica tells you what you need to know to make your trip comfortable, safe, and interesting. It tells you how to set up the all-important initial visit and provides suggestions on many sectors of business including tourism, duty-free zones, securities, investment, and a special section on financial services. We hope it will give you an appreciation of the country and help you answer the question: Do I want to do business or spend time here?

An extra bonus for those who have the time is Costa Rica's unbelievable wildlife, unspoiled jungle, and beautiful tropical island retreats. We've mentioned a smattering of these so your trip can be coupled with an adventure, a weekend retreat, or a relaxing vacation.

This book does not, and is not meant to, replace specific business books that list statistics and addresses, like the *Costa Rican Export Directory.* This is a supplement that provides the practical and personal information a businessperson needs in order to be prepared and to get through the business trip without having a mini-breakdown or, worse, being misled or ripped off.

We've done your walking for you, so you can kick start yourself into action as soon as you land.

1 The Land and the People

Costa Rica's lure stems from its temperate climate and biodiversity. This small country boasts more than 1,400 species of orchids, over 850 tropical birds, 40 semi-active volcanoes, cloud forests, and lowland jungles.

The Costa Rican government is moving to protect this valuable birthright by designating parklands and placing restrictions on industry. Businesses are now obligated to produce an environmental impact report, and projects must be designed to minimize their negative effect on the environment. The government is aggressively pushing for new, but sustainable, development and recently negotiated a regional international agreement of cooperation to implement programs that reduce the threat of global climatic change and foster renewable energy projects. Environmentally aware businesspeople will laud these moves.

The glowing picture of Costa Rica becomes even more alluring when you consider the country's stable democratic society, government commitment to socioeconomic development, high health and education standards, and long life-expectancy rates.

Costa Rica Positives

Consider the following points and you may be interested in a business trip to Costa Rica:

- Foreign policy is based on nonintervention. The country has no army and is protected by international treaties and organizations.
- Costa Rica is an active member of the World Bank and the International Monetary Fund.
- Approximately 250,000 tourists from the United States alone visit Costa Rica each year.
- There are no restrictions on capital or profit repatriation.
- Free trade zones, tax incentives, and duty exemptions have been set up for foreign manufacturers who wish to produce goods for export using Costa Rica's highly skilled and trainable work force (see chapter 8).
- Any technology can be imported as long as it meets conservation requirements.
- Almost half of Costa Rica's imports are from the United States; almost half its exports go to the United States.

Business incentives and statistics like these make Costa Rica worth a good but hard look.

Costa Rica's democratic traditions, commitment to human rights, and deserved reputation as a peace-loving nation and as a peacemaker for its sometimes unruly neighbors also make it a preferred Latin American country for business.

Note of interest: In 1987, Costa Rica's former president Oscar Arias won the Nobel Prize for Peace after he organized a regional peace plan for his Central American neighbors.

Costa Rica is unusual among Latin American countries for not having a population made up of the very wealthy and the shockingly poor, with little in between. Instead it has a large, hardworking, upwardly mobile middle class that is economically and politically influential. It also boasts a highly educated and trainable work force, a strong industrial base, a well-developed production infrastructure, and a modern communication system.

Costa Rica's constitution gives protection not just to the country's citizens but also to foreign investors. The constitution ensures that foreign investors have the same legal rights as citizens, with the exception that noncitizens cannot participate in political affairs.

As this suggests, foreign investment is not new to the country, and Costa Rica is endeavoring to keep its doors open for investment with tax incentives in

Note of interest: In the early 1990s, the United Nations announced Costa Rica had the best human development indices among developing nations. Among other statistics, life expectancy in Costa Rica is high at 75 years for males and 79 years for females, and the literacy rate is the highest in Central America at 93%.

areas such as tourism and agriculture and through the privatization of government-run industries such as banking and public works.

The growing deficit, a negative for Costa Rica, is proving a positive opportunity for entrepreneurs. Recent concern about the weighty deficit forced the government to reduce public spending. The solution was to allow private investment in public infrastructure, traditionally run by the government. In the mid 1990s, a new law was enacted that allowed private companies to construct and then exploit public works such as highways, bridges, or airports.

Most important, Costa Rica continues to hold multilateral and bilateral trade agreements with other countries, ensuring preferential access to foreign markets.

Costa Rica Negatives

Many savvy business people have lost money or simply failed in their Costa Rican business enterprises. This is partly due to the misleading notion, cultivated around the country, that it is a land of milk and honey where making a living is easy. It's also because Costa Rica attracts professional swindlers and shysters looking for easy money from full foreign pockets.

The country is renowned for being a con artist's haven, especially in the area of real estate. The naive can buy land that does not belong to the seller, that is not zoned for the intended use, or that is never registered in the buyer's name.

A related problem is that land can be expropriated by squatters or the government. This risk is intensified if the land is empty. The U.S. government distributes an eye-opening document detailing cases of expropriation, "Confiscated Property of American Citizens Overseas: Cases in Honduras, Costa Rica and Nicaragua," that is available to the public. For a copy write to the U.S. Government Printing Office, Superintendent of Documents, Congressional Sales Office, Washington DC 20402.

Another worry is that the government's commitment to sustainable ecological development can cause difficulties for the foreign entrepreneur. Tourism projects have been stopped by the felling of a tree. In one case, land was bought for a hotel that subsequently couldn't be built because turtles lay their eggs at the site during one month every second year.

External debt hampers Costa Rica's development. It is not viable for entrepreneurs to secure government funding and bank loans due to high interest rates on loans.

In 1994, a scandal rocked the Costa Rican government when the nation's oldest bank, Banco Anglo Costarricense, lost US $102 million from bad investments, insider loans, and Venezuelan bonds. The government was forced to shut down the bank, the first time a state-owned bank had been closed since Costa Rica nationalized the banks in the 1940s.

Because of incidents like this, foreign assistance is at a trickle and Costa Rica now only receives foreign loans designated to restructure the government's cumbersome bureaucracy. Less money means fewer incentives for foreign business.

In spite of these concerns, Costa Rica still rewards business people who research carefully before they commit to any project.

Note of interest: Multinational companies like Eveready, Motorola, and Panasonic have made Costa Rica their regional headquarters.

Country Profile

After the arrival of Christopher Columbus in 1502, Costa Rica remained a sparsely populated country of swampland, jungle, and inhospitable natives. It wasn't until the colony gained its independence from Spain in 1821 that settlers began to arrive in large numbers after the country's first president offered free land to Europeans who would come to plant coffee. The eventual proliferation of small coffee farms was in direct contrast to the trend in other Central American republics where a few wealthy families controlled the coffee industry. The result was that Costa Rica developed a middle class and an equitable society with land and work distributed evenly. This heritage is the basis of, and the key to understanding, Costa Rica's culture.

Recent History

During the last three decades, Costa Rica's economy has been on a roller coaster. Government policy through the 1960s and 1970s was to endeavor to become self-sufficient in industry and agriculture. Ironically, this self-sufficiency resulted in a growing need for imported fertilizer, pesticides, raw materials, and machinery. Hefty loans were received from developed nations for infrastructure projects like roads, bridges, and hydroelectric dams.

In the 1980s, when banana, coffee, and sugar prices plummeted on the world market, Costa Rica found itself in dire financial straits. Unstable neighbors like El Salvador and Nicaragua made matters worse by disrupting trade in the Central American Common Market.

Government policy through the 1980s and into the 1990s favored large industrial farms with high startup costs and minimal labor at the expense of small family farms. The sale of real estate to foreigners also gained momentum. Independent subsistence farmers, formerly the backbone of Costa Rica's economy, couldn't compete. They were forced into poverty and a jobless, sometimes homeless existence in the streets of San José. They are noticeable both by their numbers and their look of desperation.

Until recently, Costa Ricans benefited from free medical care, education, unemployment assistance, and other programs. In the mid 1990s, however, loans from developed countries became increasingly difficult to obtain. The government initiated belt-tightening measures to attract and pay off loans. This wreaked havoc on Costa Rica's social system. Poor infrastructure and overburdened health and education systems forced the government to take further economic austerity measures which, along with the government's support for foreign investment at the expense of traditional farmers, have caused a rift in Costa Rica's class structure and have fostered internal unrest.

Geography

Costa Rica is located in the geographic center of Central America. It is bordered by the Pacific to the west and the Caribbean Sea (Atlantic) to the east. From the highest peaks in Costa Rica it is possible to see both oceans at once.

The Caribbean coast is 200 km (124 mi) long and generally quite straight, but the Pacific coast stretches for 1,200 km (745 mi) and is riddled with headlands, inlets, and peninsulas. On the north border is Nicaragua and to the south is Panama.

Costa Rica's area is 51,100 square km (19,730 square mi) — about the size of West Virginia. The country is divided into seven provinces, and its regions are ecologically and climactically diverse.

> **Note of interest:** 25% of the total surface of the country is designated as protected areas; 12% of this is national parks.

Divisions

Costa Rica is divided into seven provinces, but it is also demarcated by distinct geographical areas that spill over the provincial divisions, making it difficult to get one's bearings.

The major cities in each province bear the province's name, except in Guanacaste where the major city is Liberia. The provinces are:

(a) San José. The country's largest city and capital, San José, is here, along with major industries. Its central location, easy access, and temperate climate contribute to the province's popularity. San José is mountainous and temperatures are cooler than in the coastal provinces.

(b) Alajuela is an inland province located in the middle of the northern part of the country, on the border with Nicaragua.

(c) Heredia is also on the border with Nicaragua. It stretches east nearly to the Caribbean.

(d) Puntarenas is the most important tourist region and the largest province, stretching from Panama north along the Pacific coast.

(e) Cartago is a small landlocked province, an easy day trip from San José.

(f) Guanacaste is located in the north on the Pacific side, bordering Nicaragua.

(g) Limón province runs up the country's Caribbean coast.

Three mountain ranges divide Costa Rica into five geographical areas: tropical lowlands on both coasts; north central tropical plains; Central Valley highlands; and the low northwest zone. The Central Valley is the only geographical area with a large population base. San José province is centered in the valley, with Heredia to the northeast, Cartago to the southeast, and Alajuela, northwest.

Population

Costa Rica's population is estimated at just over three million. A little over half (51%) of the citizens live in urban centers.

The Central Valley has the largest population base in Costa Rica, with two-thirds of the country's total. Population is concentrated around the capital city of San José and, to a much lesser extent, around the towns of Alajuela, Heredia, and Cartago.

People

Ninety-five percent of the population is of European descent, with the majority descending from settlers who came from Andalusia in southern Spain. There are a small number of Italians and Germans.

Approximately 7% of the above are of mixed Indian and European heritage, mostly from other Latin American countries.

Three percent of the population is Black, the descendants of men and women brought from Jamaica as laborers to build Costa Rica's railroad. The majority of the Black population lives on the Caribbean coast.

Approximately 1% of the population is Chinese, and 1% is aboriginal people who live in the Talamanca Mountains.

Note of interest: There are only 5,000 to 10,000 aboriginal people native to Costa Rica remaining in the country. When the Spanish came to the area, the spear-wielding natives were no match for the settlers and their guns. Most fought to the death; those who surrendered died of illness carried by the Spanish or were worked as slaves until their numbers dwindled. Many of those who survived intermarried with the Europeans and are now indistinguishable from the "newcomers."

Costa Ricans refer to themselves as "ticos." The name comes from their habit of using the diminutive "tico" at the end of a word, as in "un momentico," (different from the Spanish "un momentito"). The diminutive "tico" is said to have originated with the rural inhabitants.

Religion

Ninety-five percent of Costa Ricans are members of the Roman Catholic church. Freedom of worship is guaranteed in Costa Rica, and small pockets of other religions exist. Recently, there has been some growth in evangelical Protestant sects.

Politics

Costa Rica has been a sovereign democracy or republic since 1848, with power distributed among four arms of government: executive, legislative, judicial, and electoral. The president holds executive power. Open elections are held every four years, and the president cannot be elected for two consecutive terms.

There are two vice presidents and a presidential cabinet made up of 22 ministers of state who hold offices in economic, social, productivity, and cultural areas.

The legislative assembly (Asamblea Legislativa), comprising 57 delegates elected by popular vote, is responsible for drawing up the laws. Delegates serve for four years and cannot hold consecutive terms.

The 17 magistrates who form the Supreme Court of Justices are appointed by the legislative assembly. These magistrates in turn select judges for the high courts, local courts, and civil justices in different jurisdictions.

In accordance with Costa Rica's constitution, the Electoral Tribunal acts as an independent body within the republic and is responsible for organizing, running, and supervising the elections that take place every four years.

The supreme law is a written federal constitution, drafted after the country's civil war in 1948, which guarantees freedom of expression and movement and sets out the sacredness of human life and private property. The constitution established Costa Rica as a free and independent democratic republic.

Questions for the Future

Too many business people are saying that Costa Rica's nickname, the Switzerland of the Americas, is being replaced by a new name: the rip-off of the Americas. The reasons are high price tags on everything from labor to land, food, and tourism, and the promise of higher taxes.

Although workers are educated, Costa Rica has strong unions and the price of unskilled labor may be high. Factories are being moved to cheaper Central American countries like El Salvador, Honduras, and Guatemala. Couple high unemployment with government cutbacks on all social services and you've got a recipe for economic slowdown and poverty. Economists say that servicing the public debt (8.2% of Costa Rica's domestic product) is absorbing capital, driving up interest rates, and slowing the country's economic growth. Tax concessions for foreign investors are being cut each year.

Tourists complain of price gouging. For example, three entrance tickets for nonresidents to any of the country's parks cost as much as one night in a reasonably priced, four-star hotel room in any North American city. As well, a proliferation of small hotels with not enough tourists to fill the rooms makes accommodation ventures a risk for new entrepreneurs on the tourism block.

On both the Pacific and Atlantic coasts, beautiful beaches that are littered with refuse affect tourism. The consensus of many business people who work and live in Costa Rica is that although the government has done a great marketing job for the country and ecotourism, there is not much substance to it. They feel that Costa Ricans need to be educated to protect their own environment, and this step has not yet been taken.

San José, Costa Rica's capital city, is dirty, smoggy, sometimes dangerous, and has nothing to recommend it to the traveler. The country's roads are, at best, uncomfortable to drive on, and living and traveling costs are high in relation to the rest of Central America.

In spite of all these problems, Costa Rica's economic, social, and political framework makes it a safe bet. Land prices are falling, and the drop in tourism is making Costa Ricans rethink their attitude toward tourists. The government's high deficit is forcing it to do what was, until recently, unthinkable: hand over profitable public works to private enterprise. Here is where the opportunity lies for entrepreneurs with foresight and patience.

2 Opening the Door — and Keeping It Open

Preparation

If this is your first trip to check out Costa Rica's market size and the potential for your particular area of interest, you should establish a relationship with one of the country's law firms and accounting firms before you go. Your lawyer and accountant at home may have offices or affiliate offices in San José that you can contact. If not, they may have done business with firms there that you can contact, or you can ask them to find a firm and give you an introduction. Time is money, but as long as you have an introduction you are not usually charged for a first consultation.

If you can't establish contacts this way, try to locate firms in your home city that have associates in Costa Rica. Embassies, trade commissions, and your industry or professional associations will also be happy to refer you and give you contacts.

The American Chamber of Commerce (AMCHAM) in San José is an excellent source of information and will put you on to reputable contacts.

Its objectives are to foster the development of trade and investment among the private sectors of Costa Rica, the United States, and other countries. AMCHAM has offices in San José and in Florida.

The Canada Costa Rica Chamber of Commerce also acts as a liaison for government and private sector contacts. The knowledgeable staff will help you identify opportunities.

Staff at the Canadian or American consulates in San José can put you in touch with these organizations or similar groups.

Tip: Check with the Canada Costa Rica Chamber of Commerce for seminars on doing business in Costa Rica. These valuable seminars cover topics such as purchasing real estate, banking and finance, and legalities.

The Costa Rican Center for Export and Investment Promotion (Centro para la Promoción de las Exportaciones y de las Inversiones or CENPRO) assists foreign investors by supplying information on export processes and helping them structure their projects. According to CENPRO, the formula for success in Central America is to have a good distribution network and effective promotion, to maintain high product quality, to know and understand the trends of your marketplace, and to deal in hard currencies. CENPRO offers training programs and provides product and market statistics. For information call (506) 221-7166 or fax (506) 220-4754.

The Costa Rican Coalition for Development Initiatives (Coalición Costarricense de Iniciativas de Desarrollo or CINDE) promotes exporting, importing, and investment. It offers feasibility studies, new market searches, and product marketing. English-speaking staff are available at (506) 220-0366 or 220-4755, or fax (506) 220-0290 or 220-4754. CINDE also has offices in Miami and New York.

The Chamber of Representatives of Foreign Companies, Distributors and Importers (CRECEX) helps foreign businesses that wish to introduce, promote, and sell their goods and services in Costa Rica. CRECEX advises foreign companies about formalizing their business in Costa Rica and dealing with Costa Rican companies. It provides information on legal and economic issues, customs procedures, insurance, collection of payment, and import/export marketing advice. To contact CRECEX call (506) 253-0126 or fax (506) 234-2557.

PropData, a private enterprise organization, helps foreigners who are purchasing Costa Rican real estate. PropData offers a range of due diligence services such as title search and plot map studies, including searches for title encumbrances and hidden problems, possession and zoning, appraisal and market studies, and legal support. Contact PropData at (506) 233-6435 or fax (506) 255-4611.

Antonio Arreaga-Valdez is a private business consultant who helps foreigners wanting to set up business in Costa Rica. Contact him at (604) 988-5533, fax (604) 988-5559, or write to him at the Latin Export Group, P.O. Box 16076, North Vancouver, British Columbia, Canada V7J 3S9.

Tip: You will likely be doing business in San José, where there are many North Americans working as lawyers, real estate agents, and accountants. It is important to use them as your contacts since they will not have the family ties and obligations that can color a native Costa Rican's business advice. As well, there is no language barrier between North Americans, which is especially useful where contracts are concerned. In the case of real estate agents, even North American ones, it pays to be careful. Check their credentials and the length of time they have been doing business in Costa Rica before you start negotiations. Always take the contract to a reputable lawyer before you sign on the dotted line.

Letters of Introduction

Have your local law or accounting firm write a letter of introduction to its Costa Rican contact. The firm can fax this letter to the contact, or you can present it personally. If the letter is faxed for you, be sure your objective and arrival date are clearly stated.

If you don't have connections through your lawyer or accountant, you can write your own letter of introduction. If you are contacting someone recommended by AMCHAM, CINDE, or another organization, be sure to mention the name and affiliation of the person who made the recommendation.

Costa Rican firms receive many requests for meetings with newcomers and are happy to spend an hour or so discussing the local scene. Of course they hope you will actually commence your project and use them to represent you.

Tip: If you have a title — President of Tropics Corporation, or Director of Marketing — or any educational designation, don't forget to put it in your letter of introduction. Costa Ricans are impressed by education and titles.

Appointments and Contacts

Business in Latin America is done face to face — personal contact is vital — so don't be disappointed if your initial letters and faxes are not answered. A personal phone call and, later, a visit will ensure the beginnings of a relationship.

If your time is short or you believe your contact to be busy, you would do well to fax ahead and confirm when you will be telephoning to make an appointment. Also suggest two possible dates for the appointment to ensure that you get one. Don't forget to refer in your fax to your hometown contact or attach a letter of introduction from the contact.

You may prefer to visit a Costa Rican firm *after* you have familiarized yourself with local conditions, including market appraisal. You will then be able to maximize your visit.

Tip: Get further relevant referrals from each appointment. Costa Ricans love to network and welcome friends of friends or even acquaintances.

The Etiquette of Business

Many Costa Rican habits and customs are similar to those of North Americans, but remember that Costa Ricans are *not* North Americans. They have their own culture and business practices, and some of their attitudes and traits are very different.

One that is particularly difficult for business people from the United States and Canada to grasp is the concept of *mañana* (tomorrow). Many first-time business travelers go home frustrated because they do not get enough done quickly. Patience is the key. Understand that everything takes longer in Latin America.

This does not mean you can just sit and wait for your Costa Rican partner to keep the ball rolling; *you* must keep it rolling or the deal will fizzle. You or the representative that you hire (and for this reason he or she should be North American) will need to politely and patiently keep pushing for what you need done.

Before you have started a business or personal relationship with a Costa Rican, it is unlikely that he or she will return your first phone call or respond to your initial fax. This means nothing; be persistent and you will be acknowledged.

The frustration of bureaucracy and red tape is at a high level in Costa Rica. Banks can be lined up for hours, and all contracts need multiple signers with multiple signatures to be legal. Be vigilant, beware, and be patient.

Note of interest: Costa Ricans write the date with the day first, then the month, then the year.

Being on Time

Other than for lunch, the main meal of the day, ticos are often late. Their concept of time is flexible, and you may find they arrive up to half an hour late for business or social engagements. This does not mean they will accept the same from you. You must be on time, especially for luncheon.

Using Names and Titles

Costa Ricans are serious, formal people and like to be treated with respect. People you meet must be addressed by their title and a surname. Only children, family members, and close friends call each other by first names.

Education is a matter of great pride to Costa Ricans. The following degrees are used as spoken titles. No surname is needed.

- Lawyers are called *Abogado*
- Teachers are *Profesor*
- Engineers are *Ingeniero*
- Architects are *Arquitecto*
- PhDs and physicians are *Doctor* (for example, Shawn McCrea, PhD, would simply be called *Doctor*)

Tip: Make sure you use titles unless you are specifically asked not to.

People without professional titles should be addressed in Spanish with the appropriate title: Señor (Mr.), Señora (Mrs.), or Señorita (Miss) in front of their surnames.

Costa Ricans often use both their mother and father's surname. The father's surname comes first. When addressing someone verbally, it is common to use only the father's surname (e.g., Señor Roberto Arturo Fernandez Arias would be addressed as Señor Fernandez).

Women add their husband's surnames to their own name and use the surnames of their husbands (e.g., the single woman Señorita Victoria Katerina Fernandez Loewen would be addressed as Señorita Fernandez. If she married a man with the surname Cordoba, her name would be Señora Victoria Katerina Fernandez Loewen de Cordoba. She would be verbally addressed as Señora de Cordoba, or less formally as Señora Cordoba).

Family, Hierarchy, and Status

Costa Ricans believe in the equality of each and every individual, although money and family lineage determine social position. Family and national identity are particularly important concepts. This means that a Costa Rican will prefer to give business to relatives or Costa Rican associates rather than to a new-to-town foreigner. The more contacts you have, the more successful you will be.

Costa Ricans also feel morally obligated to employ and further the careers of family members — even distant ones — and their network of friends, hiring a friend or relative even if he or she isn't the best candidate for a position. Keep this in mind when you go into business with a Costa Rican partner or hire a Costa Rican to manage your affairs.

> **Note of interest:** While Latin style *machismo* (a strong sense of masculine pride) is central to the Costa Rican family, women are independent from their husbands in their own career and business matters.

Business Cards and Greetings

- Make sure your business card presents you in the highest possible position.
- Always present your business card at the time of introduction.
- Have your business cards and proposals printed in English and Spanish.
- On first meeting, Costa Ricans greet each other with a simple western-style handshake.
- Women often pat each other lightly on one shoulder rather than shaking hands. Women who know each other give a kiss on the cheek when greeting and saying good-bye.

- Men and women who are friendly may kiss on greeting and when taking leave. Men rarely if ever hug or kiss each other. Men do not back slap and embrace, though this is a common greeting in other Latin American countries.
- In the country, men tip their hats to each other in greeting rather than shaking hands.

Social Taboos

There are few social taboos in Costa Rica. Rules of polite society are similar to what we adhere to at home.

- Putting your thumb between your middle and index figure while making a fist is an obscene gesture known as "giving someone the fig."
- It is rude to close car doors loudly — including taxi doors.
- Don't put your feet up on furniture.
- Do not refer to Costa Ricans as Ricans.
- Don't pay a visit to your business associate's home without an invitation.
- Women must not wear trousers or revealing clothes.

Etiquette

- You must introduce yourself and shake hands with everyone present at a social occasion.
- Conversation should center around topics such as family and compliments about Costa Rica. The natural beauty of Costa Rica is a good subject.

- It is helpful to know the history of democracy in Costa Rica and to discuss it in an informed and positive way.
- It is acceptable to bring a gift of chocolates, quality brand liquor, or flowers (except calla lilies, which are appropriate only for funerals) if the social occasion is at a private home.

The Correct Attitude

Costa Ricans prefer to do business with people who take the time to build relationships and treat them on an equal basis. It is important to Costa Ricans that their business associates value and understand them. Open criticism is not appreciated. The establishment of a relationship is important, and compromise through discussion, not aggression, is the key to success. Costa Ricans hold personal opinions and beliefs strongly. While they will readily discuss their opinions, it can be difficult to sway them.

> **Tip:** We can't emphasize enough how important contacts are in Costa Rica. Proper introductions are the key to success.

Negotiations

- Remain formally attired by keeping your jacket (and tie) on during negotiations.

- Listen equally to everyone at the meeting; decisions are made by the group, not by one high-ranking individual.
- Discussions, patience, and trust are essential. As decisions involve a group, they are often time consuming. Do not show impatience, as it will be taken as lack of understanding.
- Informality can sometimes be mistaken for an "I am better than you" attitude. Treat everyone respectfully and equally.
- It is in poor taste to brag about wealth or your high business position.
- You will lose the deal if you demean or criticize someone publicly.

Tip: As schedules and time frames are not rigidly adhered to, expect to travel to Costa Rica several times to close a deal. You must show tolerance of this. Also be aware that late payments are part of the loose attitude toward time.

3 Basics for the Business Traveler

Language

Spanish is the official language of Costa Rica. English is the second most common language and you can usually get by with it in business and tourist situations.

Tip: Although English is widely used in commerce and industry, there are listings of interpreters, if needed, in the classified section of *Tico Times* and in telephone directories. The Canada Costa Rica Chamber of Commerce offers translation services in English, French, and Spanish at competitive rates.

Climate

Costa Rica's diverse geography results in a variety of habitats ranging from tropical dry forest and lowland rain forest to páramo (high-altitude grassland), with a corresponding difference in climatic conditions. In general, temperatures range from 14°C to 22°C (57°F to 72°F) in the high Central Valley, and from 22°C to 28°C (72°F to 82°F) in the lowlands, with slight variations between the dry and wet seasons. March and April are the warmest months and November through January is the coolest time.

The dry season usually prevails from December to April and the wet season, also called the "green season," from May to November. These seasons are clearly defined on the Pacific side of the country but are less noticeable on the Caribbean side where the precipitation is evenly distributed throughout the year.

The average daytime temperature in San José, Heredia, Cartago, and Alajuela hovers between 18°C and 22°C (64°F to 72°F) year round. Coastal areas are much warmer at around 28°C (82°F).

What to Wear

Formality and conservatism are the style for both sexes. Business travelers should pack lightweight suits as most business will be done in San José. Although the climate in the city is termed mild, a lack of air-conditioning in all but the largest, most modern hotels, and warmer daytime temperatures than northerners are used to, call for lightweight, breathable, natural fiber clothing.

In San José you will want light clothes most days, and a sweater at night. Rainwear is a safe bet no matter what the season.

Men should wear lightweight, conservative suits, plus tie, with long-sleeved business shirts. Dark colors are best.

Women should wear lightweight, conservative business suits, dresses with sleeves, or skirts and blouses with sleeves. Women must not wear trousers, shorts, or sleeveless tops for business occasions. And even if it's hot, pantyhose or stockings should be worn.

Tip: Women, if you fail to dress modestly, you will be reviled by women and pursued by men of all ages. Even when you are dressed acceptably — especially if you are blonde — men may call out or hiss at you when you walk unaccompanied down the streets of San José city. Although North American women will find this attention annoying, it is acceptable *machismo* behavior in Costa Rica and should simply be ignored.

For recreational travel out of San José, casual and resort clothing, including shorts and T-shirts, is appropriate. A light pair of pants and a long-sleeved shirt will keep the mosquitoes away at night and give you some extra protection against the mud and bugs in the jungle should you go hiking. Do not forget insect repellent.

The coasts can be oppressively hot; if you will be spending time on the Pacific or Caribbean, make sure you have something light and cool to wear, plus a change of clothing.

Visas

Americans, Canadians, and citizens of most European nations do not need tourist visas. Generally, if you have a passport, you are allowed a 90-day stay in the country.

If you don't have one of these passports, you can get a 30-day tourist card to visit Costa Rica. This card is available from travel agents or the Costa Rican consulate in your home country.

If you overstay your 30-day tourist card or 90-day passport limit, you can get an extension from most travel agencies in San José. In this case, you will need to get an exit visa and pay a nominal fine.

Citizens of certain Latin American, east European, African, and Asian countries must obtain a visa from a Costa Rican consulate and leave a refundable deposit upon entering Costa Rica.

Note: These entry regulations are subject to change; check the current rules before you go.

Tip: You should carry a copy of your passport or your tourist card with you at all times, as government authorities may ask for identification. It is wise to leave your passport in a safe at your hotel.

Health Matters

Due to the risk of cholera and other water-borne diseases, it pays to be careful what you drink and eat in Costa Rica. Many areas of Costa Rica, including San José, have safe water supplies. If you are leaving San José, watch for signs saying "agua potable" — drinking water.

Even with such assurances, though, do make sure your water is safe — that it has been boiled or bottled and that ice is made from the same. This applies even in San José city. Bottled water of good quality is available everywhere.

No particular health documents are required for travel to Costa Rica, but doctors recommend you be inoculated against typhoid, tetanus, diphtheria, hepatitis A, and polio. Bring anti-malaria pills to use if you plan to travel outside major cities. Check with your local hospital's travel clinic for up-to-date health information before you leave.

Bring any medication you may need. Although most prescription medicines are available over the counter, they are often called by different names. If you do need to buy any type of medication while you are in Costa Rica, go to the closest pharmacy (*farmacia*). Prices for imported brands are high, but you can ask the pharmacist to recommend a similar, locally made brand that will often be half the North American cost for the same drug. Make sure you know the correct dosage, and write down instructions in English. Many pharmacists will give advice on minor medical problems.

If you get any sort of cut or scrape, apply antiseptic cream as soon as possible. Germs breed faster in the humid heat than they do elsewhere. Infections often come on quickly, especially in the polluted environs of San José city. Pick up an antibiotic cream from the pharmacy at the first sign of infection.

Tip: No-see-ums (*purrujas*) can attack your feet and ankles at dusk and during the evening on some beaches, especially in the Barra del Colorado area on the Caribbean. The bites can itch and burn severely, sometimes plaguing you for days. The only preventative measure is to cover up with socks, shoes, and pants. If you develop an allergy to these bites or any others, an oral antihistamine such as Reactine will save you sleepless nights.

It is essential to use extra-strength insect repellent anywhere there are mosquitoes. Malaria and dengue fever are common in all Central American countries.

Costa Rica has a good standard of low-cost medical care, and its preventative and curative medicine is ranked highly by international medical authorities. Physicians are usually European- or North American-trained, and many speak English. Your consulate will have a list of reputable, English-speaking physicians and dentists. Your hotel can also direct you.

Tip: Both public and private health clinics have a good standard of facilities, but bureaucracy in public clinics can be time consuming. It is less tedious to use a private doctor or clinic. For emergencies and hospital services go to the Clinica Biblica in downtown San José, or to Clinica Catolica Hospital, a few minutes north of downtown.

Although medical treatment costs significantly less in Costa Rica, don't forget to check your medical insurance before you leave home to make sure you are covered. If you aren't, buy medical travel insurance.

If you need help, the emergency number in Costa Rica is 911. The call is free.

What to Bring

If you forget some of your essentials, rest assured that most things can be bought in San José, although if you prefer imported brands you will pay very high prices. Here are a few suggestions to help make things easier.

- Bring U.S. dollars or U.S.-currency traveler's checks. Canadian dollars are not widely accepted, even in San José.
- An out-of-country telephone calling card will help you keep your hotel telephone bill down.
- Bring an umbrella in the rainy season.
- Bug repellent is important (we found Cutter's Non-Scented to be the best).
- Bring toilet paper. You'll be fine if you get caught short in a five-star hotel or a fancy office building, but if you need to answer the call of nature in an airport or a shopping center you may not have the luxury of toilet paper.

Tip: Other than in five-star hotels and resorts, toilet paper is not dropped into the toilet. Because of the sewage system, toilet paper is put into an uncovered waste basket beside the toilet.

- If you are planning to explore nature, make sure you bring hiking boots, a rain jacket or poncho, suitable long pants, a long-sleeved shirt, a sun hat, and, of course, your bathing suit.

Business Hours

On weekdays, businesses and shops are open between 8:30 a.m. and 6:00 p.m. Businesses and some shops close for lunch between 12:00 noon and 2:00 p.m. Some businesses are open Saturday until noon. Tourist shops are also open on Saturdays and Sunday mornings.

Government offices are open from 8:00 a.m. to 4:00 p.m., Monday to Friday.

Banks in Costa Rica are open weekdays from 9:00 a.m. to 3:00 p.m. Some banks are also open in the evenings from 4:00 p.m. to 6:00 p.m. If you need to change money on weekends or holidays when the banks are closed, the airport exchange booth is open on Saturday, Sunday, and holidays from 7:00 a.m. to 1:00 p.m.

Currency and Credit Cards

The *colon* is the official currency of Costa Rica. The bills come in denominations of 50, 100, 500, 1,000, and 5,000, and soon there is to be a 10,000 *colon* bill. There are coins of 1, 2, 5, 10, and 20 *colones*. Each *colon* is divided into 100 *centimos,* but you will not often see any but the 25 and 50 *centimo* denominations.

The exchange rate follows the U.S. dollar. Some establishments show exchange rates and prices in U.S. currency, and U.S. money is widely accepted.

Don't depend on credit cards out of San José, as many restaurants, shops, and hotels won't accept them. In San José, many major businesses accept credit cards, but some don't; ask before you eat or shop.

Exchanging Your Money

U.S. dollars can easily be exchanged at most hotels in Costa Rica. Banks will also exchange your money but are notoriously slow.

The Canadian dollar is not widely accepted and can be difficult to exchange in hotels and in most banks except for Banex and Banco Lyon, private establishments located in the central district of San José. There is one foreign exchange house that exchanges Canadian dollars and other currencies. It is located in the shopping center beside Gran Hotel Costa Rica, Calle 3, Avenida Central in San José.

You'll often get a better rate of exchange for cash than traveler's checks.

Tip: Lines are long in banks. Make sure you go directly to the special foreign exchange counter. Don't forget your passport. Never change money in the street. Black market money changers are masters at shortchanging you.

Taxes and Tipping

Most goods and services are subject to an 11% value-added tax (the *impuesto de ventas aplicado* or IVA, pronounced like the girl's name "eva"). There is talk of the iva being raised, though this had not happened at the time of writing.

In large hotels and first-class restaurants, a 10% service charge is normally added to your bill so there is no need to tip. Be sure to check your bill, however, as smaller restaurants do not always automatically add the charge. Leave the obligatory 10% only if the service charge is not tacked on to your bill.

It is not customary to tip taxi drivers. Tip bell-boys about 100 *colones* per bag.

Bargaining

Bargaining is not expected in modern shopping malls, restaurants, hotels, department stores, and taxis. It *is* expected in markets and in the country-side. If you are buying something from a street vendor, always bargain.

Making Phone Calls

Although Costa Rica has more phones per capita than other Latin American countries, telephoning is still a slow and frustrating process. Sometimes calls just don't go through, or you will be cut off in mid-conversation. You must keep trying.

Tip: Pay phones are so frustrating that it is often best to go to your hotel or an office to make even a local call. Most pay phones are broken but not marked as such. If they are not broken there will be a long lineup to use them. Pay phones take 5-, 10-, and 20-*centimo* coins. When you hear a series of beeps, you are about to be cut off.

You can direct dial international and Costa Rican long-distance calls. Phoning your home or office can be challenging and expensive. Costa Rica's international phone rates are much higher than those in Canada or the United States. If you call from your hotel there are surcharges on top of these high rates. It is often best to call collect, or to call and ask the person you called to phone you back. Beware of hotel surcharges on any calls, even collect. To ascertain extra charges, call the front desk before you phone.

Tip: For calls to the United States, use a long-distance service like AT&T's USADirect. To make a call from your hotel, access an outside line and then dial 114. You will be connected with a U.S. operator; this is a lot cheaper than direct dial. For Canadian calling card service from a Canadian operator, dial 0-800-015-1161 (Canada Direct).

If you need phone information, or wish to make a call while in Costa Rica, the following numbers will be helpful. Check all phone numbers, as they are subject to change.

- For international information, dial 124.
- For local information, dial 113.
- For English-speaking international long-distance operators, dial 116.
- To dial long distance direct within Costa Rica, dial 011, then 506 and the number. (Costa Rica is covered under one area code, 506.)
- To dial direct to Canada or the United States, dial 011, the area code, and the number.
- To call collect or person-to-person, dial 09, then the country code (without its 0 prefix), then the area code and number.
- For telegram service, dial 123

Some other phone numbers you might need:

- Canadian Embassy: 225-0351 or 255-3522
- U.S. Embassy: 220-3939 or 220-2305
- Emergency: 911
- Instituto Costarricense de Turismo (ICT): 1-800-012-3456

Fax and telex services are available in hotels and at marked telecommunications offices called *Radiográfica* or *Telecomunicaciones Internacionales*. If you encounter difficulties sending a fax, try telephoning the number first. There are often recorded messages that announce a change in number.

Electricity

Electricity is 110 volts, the same as in North America.

You may have trouble plugging in a shaver or recharger as outlets in Costa Rica occasionally seem too small for the prongs of North American products. This is not always the case, but it can make recharging or using some appliances difficult. Most hotels don't have adapters.

Time Zones

From late March to late October (the same period that daylight saving time is in effect in North America), Costa Rica is on mountain time — GMT minus seven hours.

From November through March, Costa Rica is on central standard time — GMT minus six hours.

Holidays

Private businesses, government offices, and shops all close down on public holidays. Many businesses are closed between Christmas and New Year's Day, or during Easter Holy Week.

- New Year's Day — January 1
- Saint Joseph's Day (San José only) — March 19
- Holy Week / Easter — Date varies
- Juan Santamaría's Day — April 11

- Labor Day — May 1
- Saint Peter's and Saint Patil's Day — June 29
- Guanacaste Day — July 25
- Virgin of Los Angeles Day — August 2
- Assumption Day and Mother's Day — August 15
- Independence Day — September 15
- Discover America Day — October 12
- All Souls' Day — November 2
- Christmas Day — December 25

Carnival in Puerto Limón takes place the week prior to October 12.

Tip: Call your travel agent, the ICT, or your country's consulate to determine what businesses might be closed during religious holidays. You can also ask the consulate which holidays will fall during the time you are in the country.

News Media

All of the six local TV stations are Spanish, but most hotels have cable or satellite. Channels vary but it is possible to get CNN, Super Channel, and HBO at many hotels.

English-Language Papers

The four daily papers in Costa Rica are all Spanish. The two local English-language newspapers are weekly. *Tico Times* has a broader view than the tourist-oriented *Costa Rica Today*.

Imported English-language papers like *Miami Herald, USA Today,* and *International Herald Tribune,* as well as other newspapers and magazines including *U.S./Latin Trade* are available from hotel newsstands.

The Canada Costa Rica Chamber of Commerce produces a bimonthly English/French magazine, *Costa Rican Record,* which deals with commerce, tourism, and investment.

The American Chamber of Commerce (AMCHAM) also has a monthly English-language magazine, *Business Costa Rica.*

4 An Expedient Arrival in San José

Airlines

Flight time to Costa Rica from Miami, Los Angeles, or Houston is only two-and-a-half hours. International flights from more than 17 airlines land each day at Juan Santamaría International Airport.

American Airlines has a good network of flights from North America, flying to San José nonstop from Miami, Dallas, and Los Angeles. In North America call toll free: 1-800-433-7300.

United Airlines and Continental offer flights to Costa Rica, and LTU has charter flights from Germany. Canadian Airlines Holidays has chartered flights from Canada during winter months.

Central American airlines fly from the United States to Costa Rica. Be aware that, although they may be cheaper, they make stops in other Central American countries.

LACSA, Costa Rica's first international airline, has flights from Los Angeles, Miami, and New York, some making stops in Mexico and Central

America along the way. In North America call toll free: 1-800-225-2272.

Costa Rica also has a second international airline, Aero Costa Rica. It flies from Atlanta and Orlando with a stop in Miami. Call toll free: 1-800-494-2727.

TACA, El Salvador's airline, flies from Miami, Los Angeles, New Orleans, Houston, and Washington. All these flights make other stops. TACA also has daily flights from San José to Belize city for the ultimate getaway.

Planning Your Arrival

San José can feel warm if you've come from the cold, or cool and damp if you have come from a hot climate. It is best to wear something relatively cool and comfortable, with a sweater or light jacket tucked in your bag as a precaution.

Unless you are being picked up by your business associates, don't bother wearing business clothes. The airport is dirty and the air-conditioning is faulty and you can change into business attire at your hotel. Women can wear pants or a light jogging suit — anything except a revealing outfit — for the taxi ride to the hotel.

Arrival Forms and Customs

The flight attendants will provide you with a disembarkation card to fill in. Slip the card into the picture page of your passport or international travel document, and keep your documents in your hand or somewhere easy to access.

You are supposed to have at least US $300 and a departure ticket in your possession when you enter the country.

Costa Rican customs law permits visitors to bring in up to US $100 worth of merchandise aside from personal belongings. A maximum of six rolls of film is allowed.

Tip: Because of high duties on imported goods, you are allowed to bring into Costa Rica only goods for your own personal use. Customs officials don't want you selling these imported goods to Costa Ricans. It is unlikely you will be checked, but if you have more than two cameras or computers, make sure they are not in their original wrappings.

Arrival

After disembarking the aircraft, you must stand and wait in the immigration queuing area for foreign passports. Look before you choose your queue. Dozens of travelers line up in the center, leaving the side queues open for travelers with sharp eyes.

After you've gone through immigration, follow the sign to the baggage claim area. A directory on the wall will list your flight number and carrier with the corresponding baggage carousel number. There are free luggage trolleys against the wall. You'll also find porters who will carry your luggage for approximately US $1 per bag.

Once you've picked up your baggage, line up in one of the customs lanes. Look for the green "nothing to declare" exit for anyone who doesn't have dutiable items. If you have more than three liters of liquor, over 500 cigarettes, or imported items that are still in their new boxes, you will be asked to pay duty on those items.

Customs regulations frequently change so check for up-to-date information before you leave.

Tip: When you leave Costa Rica, you must pay a departure tax of approximately US $10. This is a good chance to get rid of your extra *colones* before you leave. You can also pay in U.S. dollars or mix the two currencies. Check at your hotel before you leave for any changes in these amounts.

Getting to the Hotel

Once you are through customs, move on to the outdoor area to get a cab. Here you will find car rental agencies, tour agencies, and a branch of ICT. Stop in for a map and information.

A cab from the airport to downtown costs approximately US $10 to US $15 depending on your destination. Cab drivers will accept U.S. dollars or *colones.* If you pay with U.S. dollars, your driver may not have or may not want to give you change.

Taxis will not take U.S. traveler's checks. If you have only traveler's checks, you will need to exchange them for *colones* or U.S. cash. There is a money exchange on the airport arrival level and it is convenient to change money here — rates are the same as at the bank.

There is an inexpensive airport bus, but it is not suitable for business travelers. There is no room for luggage, and it is usually very crowded.

The drive to the downtown hotel area of San José takes about 25 minutes from the airport in good weather. If it is raining heavily it could take up to 40 minutes.

5 Highlights of the Cities and Provinces

Costa Rica's attractions and opportunities are like the small points in a child's connect-the-dots game — sometimes confusing, distant, and diverse from each other. Information on the opportunities in the different provinces is either nonexistent, notoriously difficult to get at, or hopelessly jumbled, making it difficult to look at opportunities as a whole.

This chapter is meant to provide an overall view of what each province has to offer. It should help business travelers save valuable time as they consider business options in Costa Rica. It can also be consulted as an encapsulated guide for holidayers.

San José, the Central Valley, and Environs

More than half of the three million people who live in Costa Rica inhabit the area called the Central Valley, although it makes up only 6% of the country's surface area. The valley sits between the Talamanca and Central mountain ranges, at an altitude of 1,220 m (4,000 ft.) above sea level. The Central

Valley contains the country's capital, San José, the nearby cities of Alajuela and Heredia, and other small towns and villages. Economists predict that sometime next century this area will become one giant metropolis.

Once you leave the congested Central Valley, Costa Rica reveals itself as a rural environment of farmland, valleys, beaches, volcanoes, parks, and few towns.

San José Province

San José province has the largest population base in Costa Rica, contains the country's major metropolis and capital city, San José, and is the most developed province. It is a prime location for someone wanting to set up a service business, purchase prime real estate, or start a tourism company, including adventure tours and ecotourism.

Provincial tourist attractions include the Madame Butterfly Farm near San José, the Río Pacuare for whitewater rafting, and Chirripó National Park.

Chirripó National Park contains Costa Rica's highest mountain, Cerro Chirripó. The park also features lakes that originated in the glacial period, cloud forests, and a diverse range of flora and fauna including quetzals and other endangered species. Park facilities include an information center and marked hiking trails.

San José

San José is the capital, transportation hub, business and financial center, and geographical heart of Costa Rica. With a population of approximately 300,000, it is the only city of any size or importance to business travelers.

All roads lead to San José, and it is used as a base for business and pleasure travelers alike. Agency offices, lawyers, accountants, consulates, chambers of commerce, and business offices are located here. There is not one central business district, however (though many banks are located in the central district). If you will be spending a lot of time at a certain office, find out where it is and book your accommodation accordingly.

A Spanish city founded in 1737, San José retains little colonial charm. With its spectacular mountain backdrop, the city center should be beautiful, but it is dirty, crowded, and polluted. Potholed roads, bumper-to-bumper traffic, wild drivers, and unemployed people aimlessly roaming the streets make the city even less appealing.

Do not stay in central San José unless you have to; it is less trying to stay in the nearby suburbs.

City Patterns

San José is set out on a grid system. *Calles* (streets) run north-south. *Avenidas* (avenues) run east-west.

The center of the city is at the crossroads of Calle Central and Avenida Central. Every avenida to the south of Central is even numbered; every avenida to the north of Central is odd numbered. Every calle west of Central is even numbered; each to the east is odd numbered. Numbers are often posted on corner buildings.

Paseo Colón, the main thoroughfare, is a four-lane boulevard running east from the west side of town, becoming Avenida Central as it runs into the middle of town. Car rental agencies are located on this avenue.

The Central Market (Mercado Central) is between Calles 6 and 8, on the north side of Avenida Central. A few blocks east of the market is the Central Bank (Banco Central) and a small plaza. One block north of the small plaza is the post office, and one block south of the post office is Parque Central — you can't miss the bandstand in the middle. To the east is the Metropolitan Cathedral.

Tip: When ticos are giving you directions, they will refer to one block as "100 meters."

Three blocks east of the Central Bank is the National Theater (Teatro Nacional). It is situated in the only area that still has beautiful old colonial buildings, a reminder of Costa Rica's Spanish heritage. A few blocks east is a prominent yellow building, the National Museum (Museo Nacional). Costa Rica's

San José

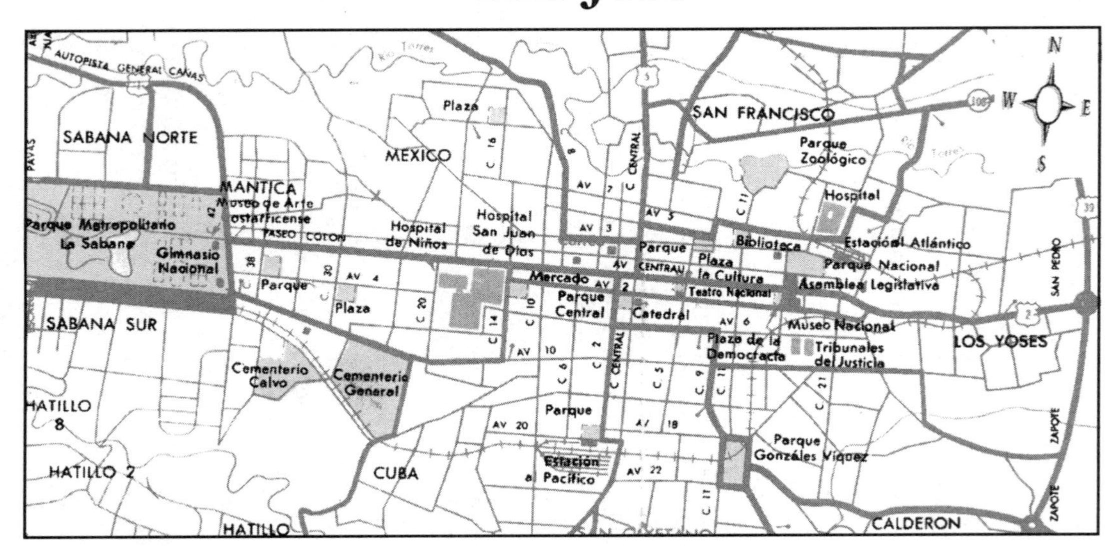

legislature, the Asamblea Legislativa, is north of the museum. If you continue north you'll see the Parque Nacional across from the National Library (Biblioteca Nacional). West of the library is the National Culture Center (CENAC). Out to the west end is another park, the Parque España.

Tip: The main office of ICT is located on the east side of the Plaza de la Cultura in San José. Pick up maps and information there or at ICT's airport office.

Alajuela Province

This spectacularly scenic inland province in the western part of the Central Valley is north and northwest of neighboring San José province. Alajuela is one of the largest and most diverse provinces. It is important for sugar processing, cattle marketing, and, increasingly, for small manufacturing. Real estate deals, both for residential and commercial use, are a possibility.

Alajuela boasts two spectacular volcanoes plus numerous hot springs. Volcán Arenal belches huge plumes of smoke and thunderous noises, attracting tourists in droves. Shops, tour agencies, small restaurants, bed and breakfasts, and hotels have proliferated in the town of La Fortuna to service the tourists drawn to this area.

Alajuela

Alajuela, in the province of the same name, is a town only 18 km (11 mi.) or 30 minutes on a busy road to the northwest of San José. It is the second largest city in Costa Rica with a population of about 50,000. Alajuela is less congested and polluted than San José and is sometimes used as a stopping point by travelers catching an early morning flight, since the international airport is only 2.5 km (1.5 mi.) southeast of the city. The convenient and comfortable airport hotel, the Hampton Inn, is located here, just a minute from the airport. There are also restaurants, bars, and movie theaters in Alajuela.

Heredia Province

Heredia is also in the Central Valley, northeast of San José. It is a coffee growing area, populated by members of Costa Rica's working class.

There are many opportunities for tourism entrepreneurs to take advantage of the province's hiking, volcanoes, and nature viewing. Braulio Carrillo National Park features two extinct volcanoes: 2,900 m (9,500 ft.) Volcán Barva is the highest point in the park, and Volcán Caño Negro is also located here. Wet forest lands around the volcanoes are good for hiking. A wide variety of mosses, orchids, and bromeliads grow here, making for ecotour opportunities. Don't miss the theme park built around a geyser that spouts 22,700 liters

(6,000 gallons) of fresh water per minute from a subterranean river.

Heredia

Founded in 1706, Heredia is a colonial city with a population of 30,000. There is one theater here and a university, the Universidad Nacional. The famous Café Britt — a working coffee farm that offers tours and a coffee museum — and a coffee research station are located close by. Heredia is only 11 km (7 mi.), approximately 20 minutes, north of San José.

Cartago Province

This small landlocked province is an easy daytrip from San José for nature lovers. It is another province of lush landscapes and towering mountains. Tourists are drawn to Volcán Irazú National Park. The Tapanti Wildlife Refuge with its hiking trails, and the Río Orosi Valley with its hot springs and scenic views, also attract tourists.

Sports enthusiasts visit Turrialba, a training ground for kayakers who practice on the rough waters of the Río Reventazón.

Cartago

The capital city of Cartago province was the capital city of Costa Rica from 1563 until 1823. It is 22 km (14 mi.) east of San José. Cartago was a historic city with interesting colonial architecture until 1910, when it was devastated by a major earthquake. It has a population of 30,000. There is nothing much of interest here — no hotels or restaurants — but the city is close to the natural wonder of Volcán Irazú.

The Pacific

Guanacaste Province

Guanacaste, Costa Rica's second-largest province, is located in the northwestern region of the country. Its major industries are tourism and cattle ranching.

Guanacaste's prime area for development is the Nicoya Peninsula, a 100-km (60-mi.) peninsula curling down into the Pacific. The Pacific side of the Nicoya Peninsula is beautiful, has all the sand and sea the tourist could want, and is called the Gold Coast for its real estate and tourism development opportunities. The Gold Coast stretches about 75 km (47 mi.) along Costa Rica's northern Pacific shore. From north to south the main beaches are Panamá, Hermosa, del Coco, Ocotal, Blanca (Flamingo), Brasilito, Conchal, Grande, and Tamarindo. Beach areas south of Tamarindo and de Sámara are less accessible.

Tip: Beware when sinking large amounts of dollars into tourism projects. There is little infrastructure in place. Only a few beaches — del Coco, Hermosa, Panamá, and Tamarindo — are accessible by paved road. Gravel or dirt roads connect the rest of the beaches.

The main tourist attractions of this province are Rincón de la Vieja National Park and Santa Rosa National Park located on the Pacific.

Liberia

Liberia, 236 km (147 mi.) from San José, is in northwestern Costa Rica. It is the capital city of Guanacaste province and the most northerly town of any interest in the country. Liberia's population numbers 21,500.

Located inland from the Pacific, it is the dry grassland capital of the cattle industry and a horse ranching center. Irrigation systems have made it possible to grow cotton and rice here.

Puntarenas Province

Puntarenas is the largest province and the most important region for Pacific Ocean beach resorts. The main portion of this province is at the southwest corner of the country, squeezed between Panama and the Pacific. A thin strip of Puntarenas then stretches up the Pacific side of Costa Rica as far as Guanacaste province.

Tip: There is still room for tourist facilities and beach resorts to be developed on the accessible and popular Pacific side. In fact, the whole southern coast in Puntarenas province is open for tourism projects.

The Puntarenas coast is rainier than the Nicoya Peninsula area, making the resort areas relatively seasonal. During the dry tourist season they are busy with sun seekers; during the wet season the sandy streets are empty. Small resort areas like Playa de Jacó (Jaco Beach) and Manuel Antonio are where the tourist action, and thus the opportunity, lies. Visitors come for swimming, surfing, sportfishing, and nature viewing, even though there are better, if smaller, beach areas dotting the ocean across the Gulf of Nicoya on the Nicoya Peninsula.

In northern Puntarenas you will find the naturally beautiful Monteverde Cloud Forest, and the province is home to numerous biological reserves.

Puntarenas

The city of Puntarenas is located at the end of a narrow peninsula, with the Gulf of Nicoya to the west and an estuary to the east. It is across from the Nicoya Peninsula and is the closest point on the Pacific Ocean to San José — 110 km (68 mi.) or two hours' drive west of the capital.

Because it is located on a peninsula, the city is only 600 m (660 yards) wide and 8 km (5 mi.) long. There are five avenidas running east-west and 60 calles running north-south.

Capital of the province, Puntarenas has a population of 43,000. Puntarenas was Costa Rica's Pacific port during the 1800s. Now it is the seasonal tourism hub for residents of the Central Valley and some foreign tourists and is the first stop on the popular Central Pacific coast. A car-passenger ferry at the northwest end of town will take you from Puntarenas to the Nicoya Peninsula. Puntarenas's scenic attraction is spoiled by pollution and street bars that are frequented by prostitutes and itinerants.

Caldera

Caldera, the Pacific port that opened in 1981, is 18 km (11 mi.) southeast of Puntarenas. It is used by cruise companies en route through the Panama Canal.

The Caribbean

Limón Province

This province, on the Caribbean side of Costa Rica, is not very developed and has not been much visited due to extremely hot, humid weather and few tourist facilities. There is room for tourism ventures, particularly in the Barra del Colorado area to the north. Ecotourism, as well as fishing and diving expeditions, are becoming popular in this area.

Limón

Capital city of the Caribbean province of the same name, Limón is 68 km (42 mi.) and a two-and-a-half hour drive from San José and sits in the Caribbean lowlands. Limón is more like an Afro-Caribbean town than part of Costa Rica. It is a banana growing and shipping port, with the occasional cruise ship stopping by. The mostly

Black population numbers about 70,000 including the inhabitants of the surrounding area.

Although it is on the Caribbean Sea, it is picturesque but undeveloped and attracts adventurers, backpackers, and surfers. In many spots the ocean is too rough for swimming, and there is no beach. Tourists tend to be uncomfortable as the city is run down and has a reputation for pickpockets. There are no scheduled domestic flights to Limón.

Avenida 2 or Market Street is the main street. The central market is in downtown Limón on Avenidas 2 and 3, Calles 3 and 4. It covers a city block.

The piers where bananas are loaded on ships is located at the south end of the port city, on Avenida 1.

The old West Indies-style city hall is located on Avenida 2 and Calle 1 across from Vargas Park. Sloths can be seen hanging from the trees in Vargas Park.

Tip: From December to February and June to August, surfers flock to Playa Bonita near Limón. Surfers say the highest waves break near coral reefs.

6 Getting Around with Ease

Unless you have the means to hire a car and chauffeur (through your hotel or an ad in *Tico Times*), getting around San José and environs is best done by taxi.

If you are off to view plantations, farms, or tourist sites, you can rent a car, rent a car and driver, or take a domestic airline.

Domestic Airlines

Costa Rica is so small that you can easily get around by road, but if you are not an adventurous and seasoned driver, you should fly the local airlines (although flying can also be an adventure, as many flights are on small planes).

Costa Rica's two domestic airlines, SANSA and Travelair, offer service within the country. SANSA flies from San José's Santamaría International Airport in Alajuela to cities throughout the country. Travelair flies from Tobías Bolaños Airport in Pavas, approximately a 10-minute drive from downtown San José. Travelair maintains higher standards than

SANSA. Tickets for both airlines can be bought at travel agents or at the respective airports.

Air taxis and charter aircraft are also easily hired. They are available through private companies such as Aero Costa Sol, which offers charter flights from San José to over 23 destinations in Costa Rica. For Aero Costa Sol information, telephone (506) 441-1444 or 441-0922, fax (506) 441-2671. In Canada or the United States, call 1-800-245-8420.

Taxis

Taxis are plentiful in Costa Rica and are the most expedient and best method of getting around, especially in San José. Most of the cars are not overly comfortable — few are air-conditioned — and drivers may try to rip you off, but they usually know how to get to your destination.

Always make sure you are entering a properly marked, legal taxi. All taxis should have yellow triangles painted on their front doors and a *maría* (meter) which registers what you owe according to time and mileage. The cars are colored red (except for airport cabs, which are orange) with a little taxi sign on the roof. You can't miss them!

Tip: Although all taxis have meters, many drivers try not to use them. If the cabbie does not turn the meter on when you enter the cab, demand that it be done by saying the Spanish word for meter, *maría*. If the driver refuses, get out of the cab. It is illegal for cab drivers not to use their meter. Drivers often demand up to four times as much money as they should when they do not use their meter. Make sure the meter is turned off as soon as you arrive at your destination. Expect to pay an extra 20% late at night.

Taxis can be rented by the hour, half day, or day, at reasonable rates. Have your hotel or tour agency arrange this. Unless you are traveling to an area that has a taxi shortage, it is more practical to take taxis as you need them and pay metered fare. Your concierge or hotel desk clerk can advise you.

Flag a cab down in the street by waving your hand and calling "Taxi." It is also possible to call for a cab by telephone. Cab companies are listed in the Yellow Pages under "taxi." If you are not fluent in Spanish, have your hotel or business associate phone for you.

Few taxi drivers speak English, but most know the names of the hotels and airport. If you are traveling to a more obscure destination, have the name and address written in Spanish by your concierge or the hotel desk clerk.

Tell or show your driver where you are going before you get in. You can tell by his response if he knows how to get there. Look in the back seat to make sure it is comfortable and clean, and don't get in unless you find it up to your standards. Unless it is raining heavily or rush hour, another taxi will soon come along. There are about 2,500 cabs in San José alone.

You may find it difficult to get a taxi in the afternoons of the rainy season or on weekdays during rush hour (7:00 a.m. to 9:00 a.m. and 4:30 p.m. to 6:30 p.m.) in San José.

In the other cities and tourist areas, taxis are also readily available. Many offer four-wheel drive. Some charge an extra fee at night.

Tips are not necessary but are sometimes expected by taxi drivers. If the service is not exceptionally good, do not comply.

Buses

Buses are popular with tourists, but they are too time-consuming and sporadic for business travelers. Buses in the city are cheap, but they are often hot, crowded, slow, and uncomfortable. The same is true for buses traveling between major cities.

Car Rentals

If you plan to travel outside San José, it may be necessary to rent a car. Try to rent a four-wheel drive if you can, as Costa Rican roads are in such bad shape. Four-wheel drive vehicles are considered top of the line by rental companies, so they are the most expensive to rent. Be careful of renting smaller models like the Subaru Justy; they are only large enough for two people and are not tough enough for the potholes in the roads.

You can rent a car from one of many car rental agencies in San José. It is difficult to find agencies outside San José.

Prices for rental vehicles are higher than in North America and vary according to the type of car. (Costa Rican rental agencies offer sedans, four-wheel drive, vans, limousines, etc.) If you will be in Costa Rica during the busy high season, make your booking in advance. **Note:** Most car rental agencies will not rent to people under the age of 25.

Tip: If you are just going to relax at a resort, the resort will provide transportation to and from San José.

Check the car at the rental company for dents, missing parts, etc. If you don't make a note of damage the car received before your rental, you may be charged for it when you return.

There are a number of rental companies to choose from (Avis, National, Hertz, Adobe, Thrifty). Agency offices are located at the airport and along the Paseo Colón on the way in to San José. To get an idea of the prices and types of vehicles available before you go, call any of these companies on the toll-free numbers.

Driving in Costa Rica

Driving in the city of San José is sheer folly. Costa Rican drivers are aggressive and don't always obey traffic rules or signs. It's difficult to navigate in the city due to heavy traffic and a proliferation of one-way and unmarked streets. Parking is impossible, and San José is notorious for car break-ins and theft.

If you are leaving San José for other parts of Costa Rica, you may want to rent a car, or car and driver (your hotel or tour agency can arrange this). Be aware that driving around Costa Rica can be a nightmare in rainy season, especially if you don't have four-wheel drive. Axle-breaking potholes are everywhere year round, and in the rain you can't see how deep they are. Bridges, often primitively constructed, can be washed out. In the wet season the roads become rivers, and mud flows are guaranteed to take a few lives. If you are not an expert driver or don't have nerves of steel, hire a car with driver for your journeys out of town.

During the dry season, driving is easier but can still be difficult. Narrow windy roads, sometimes with soft shoulders, and dust or heavy fog can make driving an all-absorbing experience. Be extra careful.

The speed limit is 80 kph (50 mph) on primary roads and 60 kph (40 mph) on secondary roads. The limit varies inside towns; watch for signs.

Driving laws and rules of the road are similar to those in Canada and the U.S. You can use your home driver's license or an international license.

- Most highway signs are international.
- Gas can be found in stations in, and at the edge of, all towns. A few are open 24 hours but, to be safe, make a habit of filling up before dark.
- Purchase roadmaps at any gas station.
- Keep small change for the toll road between San José and the international airport.
- Do not drive any distance at night.
- In the event of an accident, contact the traffic police at 221-7150 or 227-8030. If it is an emergency call 911 (the call is free).

Trains

There are only two train services available in Costa Rica. These weekday commuter trains run from Heredia to San José, and from Pavas (a suburb) to San José. They are not recommended for business travelers as they are impossibly crowded.

7 An Economic Overview for Business

The Latin American countries represent a potential market of half a billion people. As their economies stabilize, a giant consumer market will be created. Manufacturers will benefit from cheaper labor, a ready supply of natural resources, convenient shipping both east and west via the Panama Canal, similar time zones to North America's, free trade zones, and access to tax-preferred jurisdictions for company registrations. The North American Free Trade Agreement (NAFTA) between Canada, the United States, and Mexico is just the beginning of greater and more open trade opportunities with fewer or no trade barriers between these three nations and select Central and South American countries.

Trade between the United States and Latin American countries increased by 17.4% in the first quarter of 1995. Trade figures showed a 10% increase in trade between the United States and Costa Rica from 1994 to 1995. Total trade between the two countries in 1994 was US $866 million.

Economic Growth

Diversification is the key to economic progress for emerging countries. Costa Rica is no exception.

Agricultural products like sugar, coffee, cocoa, banana, and beef, and other traditional industries were the mainstays of Costa Rica's economy for decades. In fact, banana production represented 90% of the country's total exports during the early 1980s.

By the mid 1990s, traditional industries contributed less than 40% to annual export totals. Tourism had become the number one income earner for the country.

Major setbacks, such as the coffee crisis of the early 1980s and increased competition in traditional industries, wreaked havoc on Costa Rica's commodity-based economy. Inflation soared to more than 100% and unemployment almost trebled, causing a recession in 1982 that was the country's worst this century.

The stage was set for the country's economy to evolve to the next phase. Imports had to be controlled, foreign borrowing curtailed, and moves were made to diversify the economy.

Costa Rica was forced to increase efforts to attract foreign investors who would develop nontraditional businesses such as orange and teak plantations, tourism, and various manufacturing or reassembling plants.

Costa Rica has a reputation as a stable, peace-loving, democratic country. It is surrounded by unstable, often war-torn dictatorships that make it appear, in contrast, as a paradise on earth. The presence of a strong middle class and a comparatively well-educated labor force, the absence of a formal army and the existence of an enviable health insurance system appeal to foreigners who don't want too many risks surrounding their investment. The scene is set for Costa Rica to open its doors to tourism and property development.

Tariffs

Costa Rica's large middle class likes to spend its discretionary income on consumer goods. The problem has been that most consumer goods must be imported, which upsets the country's trade balance. To discourage these purchases, the government levied high tariffs on imported consumer goods and on protected industries. Before Costa Rica's admission to the General Agreement on Tariffs and Trade (GATT) in 1990, the tax on imported goods was a minimum 55%. This was later reduced to between 5% and 20%, depending on the item. However, luxury items such as cars and electronic equipment still incur taxes as high as 100%.

Tip: If you must import certain items for your project in Costa Rica, check with the government early on as to what level of tax is currently being levied. If you set up in one of Costa Rica's free trade zones, you can avoid tariffs on equipment or other imported items necessary for your manufacturing. The Temporary Admission System also allows duty-free admission for equipment and materials to be used for products exclusively for export.

Inflation

According to statistics released by the U.S. Agency for International Development (USAID), inflation in Costa Rica has ranged from a low of 9% in 1989 up to 25% in 1991, and is down to 20% in 1995. It is hoped inflation will be reduced to low double digits by the end of the 1990s.

Currency

Costa Rica allows free possession and convertibility of foreign currency to *colones* and vice versa, except for export proceeds. All foreign exchange transactions have to be settled through the Central Bank of Costa Rica. According to Central Bank regulations, certain amounts of export proceeds must be changed into Costa Rican currency.

Note: The amount that must be changed is determined by a calculation based on guidelines that change from time to time, so you should obtain current and dependable information when you need it.

The exchange rate is determined by a "managed floating system," which allows the Central Bank to intercede and manipulate, if necessary, to maintain the stability of the currency. The approximate rate of exchange at time of writing was 180 *colones* to US $1.

Average Income

By international standards, the cost of living in Costa Rica is comparatively low. The average wage has been on the rise during the mid 1990s — it is now US $2.50 an hour — and some manufacturers have started to investigate neighboring countries such as El Salvador and Guatemala, where labor is cheaper. Manufacturing companies that need skilled workers are being drawn to Costa Rica because the country's better-educated work force is able to learn new skills faster.

Employment

Unemployment has been kept under control since the mid 1980s. It has hovered between 4% and 8% during the 1990s.

Approximately half of Costa Rica's nearly three million people live in and around urban centers.

The balance lives in rural areas. The private sector employs 84% of the work force; 16% is involved in the public sector.

Tip: Costa Rica has a comparatively large and well-educated work force to draw on. Opportunities exist for personnel companies specializing in the placement of temporary employees from clerks and secretaries to light industrial and high-tech workers. The work force is evolving from semi-skilled to technically skilled. With this evolution comes opportunities for management consulting firms experienced at retraining and placing technical workers.

Foreign nationals without residency status and/or labor permits are not allowed to work in Costa Rica. Under special circumstances, foreign specialists with unique skills that local workers do not have may legally hold positions without meeting immigration requirements. Notwithstanding this anomaly in the regulations, foreign labor must not exceed 10% of a company's total number of employees or 15% of its total annual payroll.

Infrastructure

The next decade will be characterized by an infrastructure development boom in all developing nations and all aspects of infrastructure.

Since the early 1980s, access to clean water has increased from 44% to 70% of households worldwide. However, there are still one billion people without access to clean water. Costa Rica is one of the more developed Latin American countries, with 92% of the population having access to safe water.

Historically, developing countries have focused on creating jobs in the manufacturing sector. Governments are now recognizing that infrastructure development is even bigger business, with more far-reaching benefits than manufacturing.

Tip: It is anticipated that many government-controlled industries will soon be up for tender. These include electrical utilities, the telephone system, insurance, and banking. One of the first government monopolies to be broken up is the management of the ports.

The Costa Rican government acknowledges the terrible conditions of the country's roads, the inadequate international airport at San José, and the inefficient structure of government bureaucracy. It is dealing with these issues, predominantly through privatization.

Build, operate, and transfer contracts (BOTC) should be further developed in Costa Rica. The BOTC concept is that a private enterprise will build an infrastructure project needed by the country, operate it for a prearranged time period to earn revenue, then transfer it back to the government after the private developer has made its profit. For example, commercial highway developers are needed to take over the Costa Rican government department responsible for roads and highways. Developers who fix or rebuild the highways will be allowed to make them toll roads to recoup their investment. This has already been done, successfully, on the San José Airport Highway.

Note of interest: The government of Costa Rica uses New Zealand as a role model for getting its own financial house in order. Privatization played a big role in New Zealand's efforts to reduce its debt.

Costa Rica's railway has gone from bad to worse. Passenger service was closed in the early 1990s. In 1995, a Canadian consulting firm was hired by the government to assess the cargo rail service to see if it was viable for privatization. In 1994, the traffic between the two coasts exceeded 729,000 tons of cargo, including metals and agricultural produce.

Telecommunications

According to the International Telecommunication Union, Asia and Latin America, including the Caribbean region, are experiencing the greatest growth in telecommunications. Between 1992 and 1993, Asia increased its telecommunications capability by 11%. Latin America grew by 10.1%. This compares to North America's paltry 2.5% growth.

Costa Rica, with its fiber-optic network, has one of the most highly developed telecommunications systems in Central America. The Internet is a growth industry everywhere; already in Costa Rica there are as many users per capita as there are in England.

Note of interest: Early in the 21st century, Costa Rica will have some of the world's most advanced telecommunications equipment. Services planned include Integrated Services Digital Networks (ISDN), which combine voice, data, and video information on the same line, and Virtual Private Network (VPN) for faster, more efficient corporate voice and fax communications.

AT&T has been working closely with the Instituto Costarricense de Electricidad (ICE), which also oversees telecommunications, introducing new products and positioning itself for when the industry is deregulated and privatized. AT&T has also been targeting the more demanding and sophisticated corporate market.

Not all telecommunication companies have success stories. In 1987, Millicom was awarded a contract for, and invested approximately US $11 million of borrowed and shareholder funds in, the first cellular telephone network in Costa Rica. Even the World Bank thought the contract was legitimate and lent Millicom US $1 million to help develop the project. However, unions became upset with the contract, and ICE complained that the Costa Rican constitution requires the state to provide telephone service. Now Millicom says the network it installed is being expropriated by the Costa Rican government. The dispute will likely end up in the World Court of Arbitration. This is a cautionary tale for investors, and a warning that you should be sure all players are on-side before you go ahead with investment and work.

Real Estate

Real estate in Costa Rica is a major industry. In some of the Pacific coast communities, the price of property was increasing at a rate in excess of 20% per annum during the early and mid 1990s.

Locals say that you cannot go wrong buying real estate in Costa Rica, but let's take a closer look at that statement. Buying real estate should be considered a long-term investment, which requires using as much common sense, if not more, as you would back home researching a purchase. If you are speculating on short-term rapid appreciation, you are increasing your risk and you had better know what you are doing.

Foreigners and ticos have the same legal rights when investing in property — whether it is for residential use or development — unless the land being purchased is within 50 m (about 165 ft.) of the beach or within 2 km (1 mi.) of the country's border. In such cases, foreign ownership is difficult to obtain.

Tip: There are legal tactics that can be employed to deal with these exceptions. Please consult with a qualified reputable lawyer on this question, and on all aspects of property purchase, no matter how simple it may appear.

No laws regulate the activities of real estate salespeople. There are many stories of foreigners paying for a property only to find out that it was never registered in their names, or that zoning prevents them from doing whatever they had planned on doing with the property, or that it was a straight-out scam and the broker or lawyer took the money and gave the foreigner a worthless signed piece of paper. Use a lawyer and a notary to handle title searches and property transfer.

You should be aware that a deposit is not required with your offer to purchase, as it is in North America, nor can real estate brokers transfer title.

According to Carlos Arrea, partner in KPMG Legal Services, too many North Americans come to Costa Rica and decide to buy a piece of land after only being in the country two weeks. Upon their return home, they send a deposit or, worse, full payment for a property that has not been subject to proper searches or transfers. If the real estate broker and / or lawyer are crooks — and there are many — say goodbye to your money.

Tip: If you buy land, make sure you either rent it out or hire a management company so there is always someone looking after it. In Costa Rica, possession is more important than ownership and squatters are not uncommon. Absentee landowners have learned this the hard way.

Note of interest: In 1995, the real estate group ReMax sold a nonexclusive franchise to the Costa Rican real estate group Asfisa.

Consumerism

Costa Rica's large middle class and the high level of tourism present opportunities for entrepreneurs offering consumer products.

Entrepreneurs often consider buying a franchise rather than trying to reinvent the wheel. According to the United States embassy in Costa Rica, there are 32 different franchises selling US $57 million of goods and services each year, yet Costa Rica is considered underdeveloped in the area of franchise development. Fast food and automobile rental franchises are the most popular, representing 25.8% and 22.5% of the total franchise business respectively. Hotels, specialty foods, and retail clothing franchises are the next largest represented.

Pizza Hut has been a big success story in Costa Rica since it opened in 1971. In 1994 it sold 1.5 million pizzas through 24 franchises and six kiosks, grossing US $18.6 million. However, when Burger King and McDonald's came to Costa Rica, the government imposed a high tariff on french fries the restaurants imported from Canada. This was an attempt to protect local potato producers.

The high cost of real estate in the developed areas of San José and the coastal tourist communities makes it difficult for franchisees to turn a profit. After covering their fixed costs, they must pay a percentage of monthly gross revenues to the franchise headquarters.

Tip: There is a growing demand for printing services. The cost of printing in Costa Rica can be high because of import taxes on inks from the United States. A quick printing service, competitively priced with high-tech services, would do well here.

With the recent introduction of the cable networks, if your product can be effectively marketed on television, this will be your preferred way to go.

Note of interest: According to London-based Zenith Media, total billings by advertising companies in Latin America during the mid 1990s reached US $16.4 billion, double the billings of 1990. Many of the TV ads used on the Latin American versions of CNN, ESPN, or MTV are produced in the U.S. or Canada, then dubbed into Spanish.

Many of the big North American advertising companies have offices in Costa Rica. According to *U.S./Latin Trade,* Costa Rica only spends about US $68 million on advertising, based on mid-1990 figures, compared to Panama's expenditure of US $89 million or Chile's US $485 million.

Tourism

Tourism is the country's number one industry. The real estate boom of the early 1990s contributed to the tourism industry's development, as entrepreneurs bought land for tourist accommodation, particularly lower-end projects like two- or three-star hotels, bed and breakfasts, and condos.

Tip: In 1995, so many bed and breakfasts and condos were planned that an excess supply was expected to hit the market in the next few years. Good for tourists, bad for developers. Many of the projects are being developed by inexperienced hoteliers and business people. As a result, professionals in this industry should keep an eye out for failing ventures. Opportunities will exist for patient hoteliers to take over small- and medium-size hotels at substantially discounted prices during the mid to late 1990s.

Between 6,000 and 8,000 bed and breakfasts are not registered with ICT. These illegal establishments are probably not paying tax, and they may not provide an acceptable standard of service and facilities.

Tip: The real shortage, and therefore potential opportunity, is in the four- and five-star hotel category.

According to the local American Chamber of Commerce, some of the problems that must be resolved are the continued lack of government-initiated strategies and tourism planning. Costa Rica needs to market itself not just on the merit of its beaches, which are on par with other destinations, but also on the unique aspects of Costa Rica.

The country must also attract hotel chains. Sheraton used to have the Hotel Herradura in San José, Marriott opened a hotel in 1996, and the new Melia Hotel at Conchal Beach in Guanacaste province may be one of the country's best-located beach hotels.

The controversial Papagayo project is expected to alleviate the shortage of good hotels and to set a higher standard for the local industry. This immense project is in the province of Guanacaste on the Pacific. It is to include shopping centers, residential developments, numerous hotels including five-star properties, condo projects, time-share

Note of interest: Mexico's Grupo Situr, the Papagayo project's majority developer, was to open its 400-room Caribbean Village Hotel at Papagayo Gulf Tourism Development on November 15, 1995. Because of delays in local government approvals and Mexican peso problems back home, it is now thought unlikely to open before 1997.

residences, and two or three marinas. According to some locals, the project is so big it may never happen. In fact, some of the larger hotel groups pulled out of the Papagayo project in 1995, as it was taking too long to obtain government approvals.

The new international airport at Liberia was built to help the Papagayo project and all other tourism projects in Guanacaste. In time, the airport should be invaluable to property developers in this region. However, there is a catch-22. According to local hotel groups, the recently inaugurated airport will not be an attractive destination for airlines, and they will not commit to scheduled flights, until there are at least 1,000 rooms of three-star level or higher in the vicinity of the airport; but hotels are not eager to finalize building contracts until airlines have regular flights.

Tip: Canal de Tortuguero in Limón province is becoming a popular destination for travelers wanting something a little different. The canals and waterways of this region lend themselves perfectly to houseboat travel. Entrepreneurs experienced in houseboat construction and/or rentals should check it out!

Ecotourism and environmentally sustainable tourism are new forms of tourism for the 1990s and the 21st century. They target ecologically responsible travelers, adventure travelers, or people who are interested in seeing the flora and fauna of a country. Costa Rica has started catering to these interests successfully.

Tip: Despite the many potholes in the roads, Costa Rica is the perfect country to travel by motorhome. The network of highways allows you to explore the wonders of the country safely on your own, and you have the convenience of staying where you want. Motorhome rentals, and hotels/resorts offering recreation vehicle camping sites are one of the next areas of opportunity.

Opportunities await entrepreneurs prepared to develop entertainment and up-market restaurant facilities in the tourist areas, particularly in the coastal areas where evening entertainment is limited. Entrepreneurs developing consumer products for the local market should also target tourists. Trendy eateries will be of interest to both markets, as will amusement and recreation facilities.

Manufacturing

The majority of manufacturing in Costa Rica is for export. Companies that export their products are able to work in the tax-preferred free trade zones, or *zonas francas*. (See chapter 8 for more details.) Attractive tax exemptions are available to manufacturing and trade operations in these designated areas of Costa Rica. Most free trade zones are privately operated and have been developed to attract manufacturers by offering them duty and tax exemptions for importing raw materials and equipment, processed or semi-processed products, parts and components, packaging materials, machinery, spare parts, and any other goods necessary for a firm's operations and export activities.

Industries in the free trade zones range from the simplest of sandal makers to the high-tech producers of semi-conductors. Costa Rica is positioning itself for the high-tech world of the 21st century by focusing on modern technology. It is one of the world's leading software developers.

Note of interest: It is not unusual for an American manufacturer to obtain the raw materials for its product in one country, ship them to a free trade zone in Costa Rica to be assembled, (or even 75% assembled, depending on the degree of technology involved), then ship back to the United States or elsewhere for completion, inspection, and distribution. Such a company is called a "drawback" company or *maquilla.*

Although Costa Rica's work force is one of the most expensive in Central America, many North American and European manufacturers are relocating all or part of their manufacturing requirements to Costa Rica because the highly educated work force is able to take on projects requiring high skill levels.

Natural Resources

Canadian, American, and local companies are involved in mining activity in Costa Rica. Successful mining operations have concentrated on gold and limestone. Unfortunately, the largest reserves of gold are in the national parks, where the government does not allow even "controlled" mining.

Other mineral resources include bauxite, copper, coal, and sulfur.

The Costa Rican government owns all mineral rights within the country. To mine anything you need to obtain a lease or franchise from the government. The Ministry of Natural Resources, Energy, and Mines grants two kinds of permits to individuals or companies interested in mining: an exploration permit or an exploitation concession, both of which entitle you to import mining equipment with no import duties. Investors may also invest in a functioning concession through a lease or purchase.

Costa Rica's mining industry has had a checkered history. Promoters have been known to obtain the rights for a parcel of land thought to be rich in minerals, which they then flog to unsuspecting foreigners as well as locals. Lawsuits usually follow. The parties ending up with the greatest return are the lawyers and occasionally the promoters.

Before acquiring the mineral rights of an area you wish to mine, or before agreeing to any joint venture, make sure you have conducted all possible searches with the help of a reputable lawyer.

Note of interest: The government is trying to increase mining interest and in 1995 proposed a more favorable mining code.

Tip: Developing and providing new forms of energy will be growth industries of the 21st century. Costa Rica and neighboring countries are participating in clean energy joint ventures with American companies. A carbon emissions credit program was initiated in June 1995 at a San José conference. Deals totaling US $400 million were signed for biomass, geothermal, and hydroelectric projects to be carried out by American companies and Latin American countries.

Agriculture

The traditional crops of Costa Rica have been bananas, coffee, cocoa, and sugar. In the early 1980s, world prices for coffee plummeted. In 1995, European countries initiated an embargo against Costa Rican bananas to protect exports from European colonies and former colonies in Africa and the Caribbean. The impact of these fluctuations in the market was severe. To break away from their financial dependence on traditional crops and the vagaries of the banana market, farmers are planting new crops like macadamia nuts, oranges, pineapples, mangoes, strawberries, and flowers, and exploring new growing techniques, including hydroponics.

Tip: Entrepreneurs/promoters should consider hydroponics as an investment concept. With their fast-growing capacity and potential quick return on investment, hydroponic strawberries may be Costa Rica's next investment craze.

Farmers are entitled to import necessary machinery, equipment, and materials used for agriculture, exempt of all duties and surcharges. Teak plantations were a popular investment for foreigners during the mid 1990s, but local opinion said that the trees took too long to grow, therefore too long to turn a decent profit. Perhaps teak is a good investment for a patient investor. As an alternative, melina trees could be planted; they grow faster, but are not quite as hard as teak. The Cana Teca Teak farming project, based in Vancouver and San José, has diversified into nontraditional fruit and mango farming.

Forestry

In order to stop deforestation, the Costa Rican government is encouraging investment in reforestation and recycling. There are several general incentives in this area. First, companies operating under a reforestation contract may obtain a forestry tax credit certificate (CAF), which is a registered security issued by the government that can be negotiated or used to pay any kind of taxes.

Companies operating under a reforestation contract but not benefiting from the CAF incentives have the following tax incentives:

- 100% land tax exemption
- 100% uncultivated land tax exemption
- up to 100% income tax exemption on the income produced from the harvest of a plantation
- 100% exemption on import duties on equipment, machinery, and vehicles used in forestry

Costa Rica's approach to recycling is successfully represented in the Tropical Natural Fibres Company in San José. It produces paper products from recycled banana plant fiber. One percent of each sale goes toward a scholarship fund to support young leaders from Latin America to study sustainable agriculture at Earth University in San José, Central and South America's leading learning institution in environmental issues and sustainable agriculture in the tropics.

Aquaculture

Costa Rica boasts two of the best sport fishing coasts in the world, but these days nobody wants to fish for a living. There have been some aquaculture projects where fish are farm raised, and this can be effective for producing everything from shrimp to crayfish.

Fishers are entitled to import necessary machinery, equipment, and materials used for commercial fishing, exempt of all duties and surcharges.

Tip: In view of the high cost of certain seafood in Costa Rica (e.g., US $40 a pound for large prawns), aquaculture ventures to satisfy the domestic market could provide excellent opportunities. Aquaculture limited partnerships (where the entrepreneur raises capital for a project by selling interests in his or her venture to limited partners) have been sold successfully in other countries. Australia has used limited partnerships successfully to fund aquaculture projects across that country and in Indonesia.

8 Free Trade Zones

Costa Rica's free trade zones, regulated industrial parks located around the country, are the main tools in the government's strategy to attract foreign investors. In these zones, local and foreign companies develop and run manufacturing facilities where finished or semifinished goods are produced for export. The investors, in turn, receive significant tax incentives. Costa Rica gains a skilled, employed work force; increased consumer spending and economic activity; and economic diversification.

Companies established in a free trade zone may also receive the benefit of Costa Rica's preferential access to other countries like the United States, Chile, Mexico, and most Caribbean nations. For example, the B.E.S.-Taiwan Free Zone owned by the Taiwanese government is located near the Juan Santamaría International Airport. The government in Taipei encourages Taiwanese companies to use this free trade zone and take advantage of Costa Rica's preferred trading status with many other countries.

Another benefit of locating in a free trade zone is that it makes life easier for a foreign entrepreneur, since most of the zones have an infrastructure in place. Some provide child care and medical facilities; other provide labor recruitment and training centers. There are usually banks and postal services, and security patrols guard the zones.

At the time of writing, special free trade zones were located at Alajuela, Cartago, Heredia, Limón, Moín, Puntarenas, San José, and Santa Rosa. A number of new zones have been proposed, testimony to the concept's popularity.

There are six types of companies that can be established in a free trade zone:

(a) Export processing industries

(b) Trading companies distributing nontraditional products

(c) Service companies providing services to export-producing or export-marketing companies

(d) Management firms administering the free trade zones

(e) Individuals or corporations dedicated to scientific research that contributes to the improvement of technology in Costa Rica

(f) Boat construction, repair, and maintenance industries providing and operating drydocking facilities, shipwright services, and similar work

Free Trade Zone Incentive System

Companies operating in a free trade zone are entitled to the many tax incentives, including exemption from payment of all taxes and consular fees relating to the importation of raw materials, processed or semiprocessed products, components and parts, packing materials, and all other merchandise and goods required for the firm's operations and export activities.

They are also exempt from all types of import taxes and duties on equipment, machinery, and vehicles imported to assist with the operation, production, administration, and / or transportation requirements of the venture; all taxes and fees on lubricants imported for the operation of the business; and from all taxes associated with the export or re-export of products.

A 10-year exemption exists, effective upon initiating operations, from taxes on net capital and assets, property, and real estate transfers as well as exemption from sales and consumption tax on the purchase of goods and services.

Other exemptions exist depending on which zone companies are located in and how they are located. Check with the Center for Export and Investment Promotion (CENPRO), the Costa Rican Coalition for Development Initiatives (CINDE), or a local qualified lawyer to find out which zone currently has the best tax incentives combined with the necessary infrastructure appropriate for your project. Some zones are not as developed as others, so obtain up-to-date advice on the zones you are considering.

Companies in the free trade zones are not obliged to send foreign exchange currency earned from sales to foreign markets to the Central Bank of Costa Rica. Instead they can manage their foreign exchange currency with flexibility and will be allowed to repatriate capital, as well as pay for licenses, commissions, royalties, and imports at their own discretion.

Banking and customs services are located in free trade zones for quick import/export procedures. They offer on-site, simplified customs inspection and clearance; automatic exemption from sales and consumer taxes; exemption from all export taxes associated with the export or re-export of their products; and exemption from all export taxes for the re-export of equipment and machinery used in the production process.

Tip: Within the free trade zones, opportunities abound for service companies such as freight forwarders, customs brokers, insurers, and other related industries.

Companies classified as export-processing or service industries can sell up to 40% of their total production in the local Costa Rican market. Commercial relationships between companies operating within a free trade zone and companies operating outside the zone but within Costa Rica are considered import-export relationships, so the free trade zone product "exported" into Costa Rican territory is subject to the same levies and import duties as merchandise entering Costa Rica directly from abroad. However, the import-export relationship will qualify for export incentives.

Although still under the umbrella of Costa Rican law, business conducted in the free trade zones is less restricted, and the zones are the most popular investment locations in Costa Rica. They will help take the country's economy into the 21st century.

Contact CINDE for more detailed information and trade regulations affecting the free trade zones.

Note of interest: CINDE is a group of private sector leaders working in association with the government to actively promote investment in Costa Rica. CINDE offices are located in San José, Miami, and New York; Costa Rica's ambassadors in most countries have information on CINDE.

Drawback Companies

Drawback or temporary admission (*maquilla*) companies import piece goods and components for assembly in Costa Rica, then export the finished goods.

Benefits to drawback companies are similar to those for companies operating within a free trade zone, including total exemption from sales and excise taxes and from export taxes.

Finished goods must be exported, except for a wastage factor that is negotiated with customs. Benefits are granted for periods of five years, but can be renewed.

Setting Up Your Business

There are four types of legal structure used for business ventures in Costa Rica: corporation (*sociedad anónima* or *S.A.*); limited liability company (*sociedad de responsabilidad limitada* or *R.L.*); limited partnership (*sociedad en comandita simple*); and general partnership (*sociedad en nombre colectivo*).

Corporation *(Sociedad Anónima)*

This is the preferred legal structure due to its flexibility. Since local laws define a corporation as a bilateral agreement, it must be formed by at least two parties. However, immediately after formation of the company, all the shares of stock may be legally owned by a single party.

Founding parties (and any shareholders) may be physical individuals, registered business concerns of any nature, or a combination of individuals and businesses, regardless of citizenship and residence.

The cost of incorporating ranges from US $500 to US $700 for companies with share capital of between US $10 and US $100. Costs increase according to the amount of share capital.

The corporate name must be in Spanish and every corporation must have a board of directors comprised of a minimum of three individuals to hold the positions of president, secretary, and treasurer. Additional board members may be appointed at any time.

As the legal representative of the corporation, the president must hold full powers of attorney. However, another director or directors, as well as managers and outside individuals, may hold powers of attorney of any kind to act individually or jointly on behalf of the company. These powers of attorney (including those held by the president) may be limited or restricted by several means to meet the company's internal controls.

If you are giving your lawyer signing authority for your corporation, ensure there are limits to his or her power. Make sure the lawyer is independent and not associated in any way with a local business partner or associate involved in the business. Read the fine print. If it is in Spanish, have an independent lawyer translate it so you can be sure there is not a second interpretation of the meaning or intent.

Limited Liability Company
(Sociedad de Responsabilidad Limitada)

The incorporation procedure and costs for a limited liability company is similar to those for a corporation, except that in an LLC the share capital is divided into "quotas" as opposed to shares. Unless specially provided otherwise, quotas may be transferred only with the unanimous consent of all partners.

An LLC is run by one or more managers or assistant managers who hold powers of attorney as provided for in the articles of incorporation and who do not have to be owners of the company.

Limited Partnership and General Partnership

Limited partnership and general partnership are seldom used in Costa Rica. Formation procedures are basically the same as for a corporation, although much simpler. The disadvantage of a limited partnership is the strong personal involvement of the parties, particularly in relation to liabilities and management.

Other Forms of Business Entities

Foreign companies may conduct business in Costa Rica through branches of their parent company, provided that certain requirements are satisfied. Included in these requirements is the preparation of a formal statement confirming that the branch shall be subject to Costa Rican laws and jurisdiction in activities performed in the country. The parent company must submit a waiver of the laws of its domestic jurisdiction.

Foreign companies may transfer their legal domicile to Costa Rica if their articles of incorporation allow such a transfer. Note that transfer of the legal domicile does not mean the parent company has dissolved. It continues operating under the laws and jurisdiction of its original legal domicile.

Note: Rules have a habit of changing so please consult with a reputable local lawyer at the appropriate time. During the late 1990s, as Costa Rica refines its legal system and relaxes its regulatory controls, there will be many changes in corporate law, banking, and insurance.

From our personal experience we can recommend Carlos Arrea or Juan Carlos Chavarria, KPMG Legal Services, to help with these details. Contact them in San José by phoning (506) 220-1366 or faxing (506) 296-0269. KPMG Legal Services is a division of the KPMG accounting group, which can be reached at the same phone number. On KPMG's accounting side, we recommend Carlos Quiros. KPMG is the world's largest accounting group, with offices in most countries.

Income Tax

According to KPMG, Costa Rica has a "territorial tax system." This means that individuals or corporations are only responsible for paying tax on income or profits derived from Costa Rican sources within the country. Any and all income derived from the following is considered taxable:

(a) Real estate transactions settled in Costa Rica

(b) Assets, goods, and rights invested or used in the country

(c) Commercial, industrial, agricultural, and other activities performed within the country

Similar to most tax systems, deductions for expenses necessary to produce taxable income may be deducted by corporations from their gross income. Tax authorities may disallow deductions if they are not considered necessary or if they are excessive or unreasonable. They will also disallow deductions if you don't have the proper documentation supporting the expense or if they relate to another tax year.

The Costa Rican financial year starts October 1 and ends September 30. If you establish a local subsidiary or branch of a foreign company in Costa Rica, you may use the financial year of your parent company. A completed tax return must be filed within two months of your company's financial year end.

Unfortunately for the government, tax authorities do not have an effective system to collect tax or keep track of it. This has allowed many corporations to avoid paying the full tax they owe. Measures are being introduced by the tax authorities to force companies to pay up, although it is unlikely the new regulations will have any bite for a period of time.

Tax Treaties

Although Costa Rica has never been in the same class as other well-known preferred tax jurisdiction, individuals and corporations have been "hiding" money in Costa Rica for years to avoid paying taxes on it in their home country. The introduction of tax treaties would put a stop to this.

Costa Rica has signed a tax treaty with Romania. According to tax authorities it was signed to avoid double taxation. Other people think it may be the thin edge of the wedge and could be the start of more tax treaties with other countries.

There is also a tax information exchange agreement (TIEA) between the United States and Costa Rica, an attempt by the United States to catch Americans who don't pay tax on their worldwide income.

Import Duties

Import duties are outlined in the Tariff Code. All goods are allocated a number and a classification for tax calculation purposes.

Import duties are never less than 5% and do not normally exceed 20%, although duties on luxury goods can exceed 100%.

Employment Incentives

The payroll payback agreement offers employers of Costa Ricans in manufacturing and production jobs a rebate to compensate in part for wages paid to workers. Payroll payback agreements are designed for a five-year period during which the employer receives rebates of 15%, 13%, 11%, 9%, and 7%, respectively, for wages paid during that period.

Training incentive is a program that will train workers for up to three months prior to, or during, their tenure with the company. The program also pays workers minimum salaries during the training period.

Export-Oriented Incentives

Companies exporting nontraditional products out of Costa Rica that are not covered under bilateral agreements are entitled to the following benefits:

- Exemption on a percentage of import duties on raw materials, components, machinery, and equipment based on the level of export sales
- Tax credit certificates (CATS), bearer securities issued by the Central Bank of Costa Rica, for up to 10.5% of the export FOB value. These certificates (which represent a direct subsidy) may be used 18 months after the date of issue and are valid for 24 months after maturity.

Matured CATs are used to pay any type of tax or may be traded at a discount at the local stock exchange before or after maturity. (**Note**: CATs are no longer granted to new export contracts.)

- Total exemption from export taxes
- No restrictions on sales to local market
- Income tax exemption in proportion to export sales
- Exemption on a percentage of local sales and excise taxes, based on the level of export sales
- Streamlined procedure through the central customs office to expedite customs service

Taxpayers who acquire shares of stock in a qualifying export company may take a 50% tax deduction on the purchase. The shares have to be purchased through a stock exchange, and the deduction cannot exceed 25% of the investor's net taxable income. The shares must be kept in an escrow account, either at a state-owned bank or a local stock exchange, for a minimum period of three years.

Note of interest: Export contract incentives were implemented in 1984 and were to be available only for a limited time. A local accountant or lawyer will be able to tell you if these incentives are still available and if you qualify for them.

Free Trade Agreements

Costa Rica has been a member of the Central American Common Market (CACM) since 1963. The other CACM countries are Nicaragua, Honduras, El Salvador, and Guatemala. Costa Rica also has trade agreements with Panama and Dominican Republic.

Tip: If you are manufacturing in a Costa Rican free trade zone and shipping to or from a CACM member country, you will incur no duties.

Note of interest: In 1994, Costa Rica created a NAFTA-like arrangement with Mexico. This agreement allows for the free flow of approximately 12,000 different products between the two countries, incurring no duties or tariffs. This represents 85% of the total trade between the two countries. The agreement is anticipated to cover all goods by the year 2005.

9 Banks, Investments, and Financial Services Opportunities

Banking

Costa Rica's banking industry is a monopoly controlled by the government. Since 1948 it has been against the law to deposit money in any financial institution other than a national bank controlled by the state. Recently, however, the World Bank has been encouraging more openness and transparency in Costa Rica's banking industry, and privatization of the banks is imminent.

At time of writing, there were three state-owned commercial banks, two service banks created by law, 23 private banks including two cooperatives, and almost 40 finance companies. Twelve months earlier there were only 17 private banks. In anticipation of deregulation of the banking industry, foreign banks are establishing a presence in Costa Rica.

The Central Bank

The Central Bank of Costa Rica (Banco Central de Costa Rica, or BCCR), established in 1948, developed the industry's legal infrastructure and supervises the country's banking operations. The Central Bank is the only issuer of currency and is responsible for credit and foreign exchange policies. It determines economic policy and dictates how much currency is in circulation.

Note of interest: Institutions and organizations from around the world have helped Costa Rica become more productive and financially viable. Groups such as the World Bank, the U.S. Agency for International Development, the Inter-American Development Bank, and the Central American Bank for Economic Integration have used the Central Bank as their vehicle to provide debt capital or joint venture equity funds for local corporations. This increased liquidity in the capital markets ensures that there is sufficient local funding available for businesses to grow.

State Banks

Under the current Costa Rican constitution, state banks have an absolute monopoly on checking and savings accounts in any currency. The banking system is basically reliable but inefficient, a situation which is expected to improve after bank deregulation.

Private Commercial Banks

The 23 private banks are positioning themselves in anticipation of bank deregulation. Their growth has been severely slowed by their inability to legally offer checking or savings accounts. Instead, they can provide letters of credit, working capital finance, foreign exchange transactions, wire transfer services, and most other banking functions. Some banks in Miami, other American gateway cities, or Caribbean tax-preferred jurisdictions such as Grand Cayman offer private banking facilities for wealthy Costa Ricans who can afford to travel out of the country to deposit their money.

Note of interest: According to locals, it can take as long as 45 days to clear a check through the state-owned bank network. However, if you bank with one of the private commercial banks with offices elsewhere, in Miami or Grand Cayman for example, you can clear a check and have the proceeds wired back to you within 10 days.

The international banking community is keeping an eye on Costa Rica's progress at deregulating the banks. The Bank of Nova Scotia, convinced of the opportunities, expanded its Caribbean operations in 1996 and opened a branch in San José. Foreign banks with a good network in the Caribbean and Miami should seriously consider Costa Rica as their next stage of expansion.

Setting Up a Bank

Private commercial banks are set up as either corporations or as cooperatives (limited liability companies or *R.L.s*). The two cooperatives are Banco Cooperativo Costarricense R.L. and Banco Federado R.L. For either structure, the minimum capital required to begin operations is 300 million *colones* (US $1,666,000).

As we prepared this book, there was considerable disagreement about the deregulation of banks, particularly the smaller institutions. Critics of the new banking law claim it isn't strict enough in its regulation of the financial system, and they argue that smaller banks should not be allowed to offer checking accounts. It has also been proposed that the capital requirements be increased to one billion *colones*.

Other Banks

There are two banks that were created by law to satisfy particular requirements.

The Mortgage Bank (Banco Hipotecario de la Vivienda or BANHVI) was created as a source of home financing for low-income earners. The Costa Rican government allocates a specific amount of public funds to the bank.

The Popular Bank (Banco Popular y de Desarrollo Comunal) is funded by the national payroll. Every employee pays a mandatory deduction from his or her paycheck; this contribution goes to buy shares in the Popular Bank. The bank, in turn, provides loans to small business people needing startup capital.

Finance Companies

Finance companies represent a small portion of the total financial community, but they do play an important role. Their core business is to provide financing to corporations and individuals. They are also allowed to provide some of the same services as banks.

To set up a finance company you need available registered capital in the amount of 60 million *colones* (US $333,000). The company must be registered with the Banking Audit Bureau.

Interest rates in Costa Rica have been quite high since the currency was floated in 1992. Depositors were earning as much as 30% in local currency, but if investors wished to convert their *colones* to U.S. dollars, they made nothing or even lost money. Borrowers have had to face interest rates as high as 45%.

Securities Market

Costa Rica's stock market (Bolsa Nacional de Valores) has evolved from a quiet, almost dormant, exchange to the largest in Central America, with approximately US $30 million of daily trading.

The Bolsa dates back to the end of the civil war when it was known as the Commercial Stock Exchange. However, due to lack of interest, it died after one year. It was resurrected again in 1973 under its present name. Its market capitalization in 1995 was approximately US $8 billion.

Tip: Securities companies from the United States have been watching the slow but steady growth of this industry for years. Now is the time to take a proactive role in this potentially high-growth industry. The local market will need companies to help computerize trading, set up custodial and backroom administration, and provide good promoters and brokers to help develop this industry.

Opportunities exist for investors in nontraditional industries such as tourism, or in new agricultural products like teak, dried flowers and ornamental plants, hydroponic fruits and vegetables, and macadamia nuts. The deregulation of industries ranging from telecommunications to ports management will create investment and underwriting opportunities on the Bolsa.

In 1990, the Securities Commission (Comisión Nacional de Valores) agreed that within two years there would be an independent agency in Costa Rica that would assess and rate financial instruments and their issuers, similar to companies like Moody's or Standard and Poors in the United States. There was opposition to this proposal, so it wasn't until 1995 that a company called Classification of Central American Stocks (CLASE) was appointed for this purpose. At the time of writing, because of problems in Mexico, the company had not yet set up in Costa Rica.

Until CLASE is in place, the Securities Commission has appointed a four-member panel to commence the risk appraisal system. This Ratings Commission rates debt issues based on the creditworthiness of the issuers. Ratings go from AA, which is the best, down to C (considered speculative), D (implies that payments of interest or capital have been suspended), and E (no valid information has been provided to assess the instrument).

There is a plan to create one Central American regional stock market with one legal framework, a central securities depository, and a computer link that would allow all markets to trade simultaneously. This would allow institutional investors to analyze all the companies of Central America on the same basis, using standardized research information. Increased disclosure and greater efficiency will help attract both institutional and individual investors.

With the development of stock exchanges in Central America, there are opportunities everywhere for companies in related industries. Law firms are helping to formulate a uniform legal framework. Accountants are setting up accounting standards. Computer companies are designing the software and hardware requirements for each country and the thousands of firms participating. The level of investment research needs to be improved.

Electronic Exchange

The Bolsa Nacional de Valores has enjoyed above-average growth during the mid 1990s. However, its new cousin, the Electronic Exchange (Bolsa Electronica de Valores), has far out paced it in annual growth since it began operations in April 1993.

The Bolsa Electronica operates in the most important sectors of the financial community:

(a) Debt instruments. These securities represent the largest portion of total trading volume in the market. The main issuers of the bonds are the National Treasury, the Central Bank, the Popular Bank, and the state-owned commercial banks. Private banks and financial institutions are also allowed to issue this type of security. As with any debt instrument, the market value of these securities is based on term to maturity, current interest rates, and the quality of the issuer.

(b) Variable interest rate instruments. This category involves common and preferred stock issued as payment for capital stock increases in private corporations.

(c) Commercial paper. These securities represent unconditional payment obligations of borrowed capital, plus fixed or variable interest rates. Similar to other debt instruments, they are offered by commercial enterprises rather than government agencies or banks.

Commodity Exchange

The Commodity Exchange (Bolsa de Productos-Agropecuarios) started operations on August 31, 1992. Its main objective is to serve as a public means of acquisition and sale of agricultural goods. Transactions are executed by brokerage firms, which operate through concessions acquired from the Commodity Exchange. These brokerage firms are the only entities authorized to carry out transactions.

Bond Market

The Mexican currency crisis had a giant impact on Mexico's bond market and it tarred all other Latin American bond markets with the same brush.

Immediately prior to the Mexican crisis of December 1994, investors had become carried away with what appeared to be the alternative to southeast Asia as the new growth region of the world. Fortunately, there were few institutional investors in Costa Rica at the time of the Mexican debacle. New investors are now more selective and thorough with their research before committing their own or their clients' funds to Latin American investments.

Costa Rica does not have any locally registered mutual funds, but that doesn't stop the local investors from investing. Brokers from Miami, representing companies such as Merrill Lynch, come to Costa Rica every two months to wine and dine potential investors and clients. Mutual funds have increased in popularity and are the preferred investment for many wealthy Costa Ricans. They invest their money through Miami and leave it in the hands of their investment adviser and the mutual fund managers.

"Central American Venture Capital Funds" should be the next product developed by mutual fund managers. These would be a diversified portfolio of new projects in different industries located throughout Central America. They could be an excellent way for local entrepreneurs to raise capital for projects while allowing investors to participate in a diversified portfolio of investments rather than taking a flier on just one company.

"Infrastructure Funds" are another possible product for development by local investment managers.

These funds would raise capital for infrastructure development to help remove the financial burden from the government. Telecommunications, power generation, port management, and highway construction all lend themselves perfectly to the concept (similar to build, operate, and transfer contracts described in chapter 7). User fees would be charged, creating a cash flow and profit for the investors. Retail and institutional investors funding the projects could liquidate their investment either when it is listed on the local (or Central American Regional) Bolsa, or sold to another investor on secondary markets.

Investing directly in Costa Rica's, or any emerging country's, stock market is a tricky business. Time delays in buy and sell orders and the dearth of qualified, up-to-date research make it difficult.

Tip: Investors wanting to share in the exciting growth of stock markets in this region should use unit trusts or mutual funds registered in their home country but managed by experts with extensive experience in the temperamental and volatile markets of Latin America.

Investors in equities, particularly in emerging countries, must not be concerned by short-term volatility. If the fundamentals of an investment during a market correction are the same as they were at the time of investing, the best strategy is to invest more. This may not be easy, but it takes advantage of an important method of managing risk: dollar cost averaging. Equity investing should be considered a medium- to long-term proposition.

Investing in Latin American mutual funds is a conservative alternative to investing directly in one project or company. Your mutual fund will be invested in a whole range of companies in different industries and different Latin American countries.

Alternatively, emerging market funds are a less volatile alternative to investing only in Latin American countries. The manager of such a fund will look for good investment opportunities in emerging markets anywhere around the globe. Not being restricted to a geographical or political region allows greater diversification for the portfolio and, in turn, less volatility.

There are a number of top quality fund managers offering Latin American and emerging market funds. Some are listed below:

(a) Sir John Templeton pioneered the concept of investing in emerging markets and his Templeton Emerging Market Funds, available in most developed countries, have traditionally been top performers.

(b) Peter Gruber of Globalvest in Berkeley, California, is considered the world's leading specialist Latin American money manager.

His expertise can be obtained through AGF's 20/20 Latin America Fund.

(c) The Rothschild and Schroder groups, both international investment companies and with over 150 years' combined experience in Latin America, have teamed up with Kerr Neilson of Platinum Asset Management to form Canada's Global Strategy Latin America Fund.

(d) Trimark's America's Fund is one of the most conservative ways to participate in growth opportunities in Latin America.

Life Insurance

Buy a life insurance policy from the wrong company in Costa Rica and you will end up in jail.

Costa Rica's insurance industry has been a government monopoly since 1924. It is against the law for a Costa Rican to buy an insurance policy from any company other than the Instituto Nacional de Seguros (INS). Not surprisingly, the INS sells a lot of insurance and is one of Latin America's largest insurance companies.

There is serious discussion of privatizing Costa Rica's insurance industry. Already, European and North American underwriters are setting up branch offices in anticipation. The INS will have a tough time competing for business on a level playing field if the insurance industry is privatized or deregulated. Its investment portfolio is not the most imaginative, focusing predominantly on government-backed bonds.

The type of insurance being sold in Costa Rica is not too different from what has been available in other countries. Whole life and permanent insurance have been the backbone of INS's life insurance portfolio. INS uses the standard global reinsurers, including Lloyd's, spreading risk and reducing its exposure to any particular liability.

Tip: With the pending deregulation of the insurance industry and the evolution of the local stock market, opportunities will soon be created. New insurers should develop market-linked life insurance policies that will outperform any of these government-backed whole life policies. Life insurance companies need to be positioning themselves in Costa Rica now!

10 Where to Stay... and Some Adventures

Hotel Listings

We have given hotels up to 5-star ratings for their amenities: pools, spas, health clubs, conference facilities, and casinos. They are usually large hotels as smaller properties don't have the space for these things. There are few 5-star accommodations in Costa Rica, and those that are rated as such are not of the standard of cleanliness and service that world travelers have come to expect. This is apparent in both city hotels and beach resorts. Prices are not high, and they are less than North American rates, but value for money is not great when you compare Costa Rica to other Central American destinations.

Tip: Costa Rican hotel rates are quoted in *colones,* but you will sometimes be charged in U.S. dollars. If your bill is in U.S. dollars, check the exchange rate. If the hotel has not made a fair conversion, insist on being charged in *colones*.

Hotel rates vary, especially in and around San José. Five-star hotels usually charge upward of US $150 for a deluxe double room and can go as high as US $2,000 for a suite. Local chains, like the 5-star Camino Real and 4-star Holiday Inn, are about the same price and standard as they would be elsewhere.

Three-star hotels charge from US $50 to over US $100, and rates for a 4-star range from US $70 to around US $250. Suites run upward of US $200 (not including tax and service charges). Prices are a shade lower in the "green season," and many hotels will be relatively empty during this rainy, less popular time of year.

Although there are many 1- and 2-star hotels offering rooms for as low as US $20, we did not list many as, other than bed and breakfasts, they are usually tiny, dirty, and cockroach-ridden or infested with fleas. We did not list small bed and breakfasts, as many have no facilities for business travelers. Please contact ICT or your travel agent for an updated list of bed and breakfasts.

The 11% value-added tax (IVA) is applied to most goods and services. Hotels are subject to an additional 3% tourist tax. When you make your reservations ask if the taxes are included in the price quoted. Prices are subject to change, so please check with your travel agent when booking.

Tip: A Costa Rican travel agent, the airline, or your agent at home can often find packages that are cheaper than the daily room rate.

Hotels that we specially recommend are noted. Five-star accommodation is noted *****. Four stars (****) indicate older and smaller hotels, but still with reasonable facilities. Three stars (***) indicate more moderately priced accommodation with even fewer facilities.

Note that street addresses are not always given by building number — sometimes they are given by the nearest street intersections. Some hotels use post office box numbers (*apartado postal* or apdo.) for mailing addresses; others don't. Smaller hotels in the country often have a simple description for an address.

San José

With a few exceptions, even the nicer hotels in central San José can be noisy due to incessant traffic, and other than in the revamped mansion-style hotels, rooms are very small. When you check in, ask for a quiet room away from the street. Centro Colón and the other suburbs that ring central San José are much nicer, less polluted, and quieter.

Hotel Europa Zurqui *****

Apartado 72-1000, San José
Tel: (506) 257-3257
Fax: (506) 221-3976
Toll free in the U.S. and Canada: 1-800-223-6764

One of the better luxury hotels in downtown San José with 120 rooms, 2 pools, casino, conference center, secretarial services, spa, restaurant and bars, art gallery, and gift shop.

Aurola Holiday Inn ****

Apartado 7802-1000, San José
(Avenida 5, Calle 5)
Tel: (506) 233-7233
Fax: (506) 255-1036
Toll free in the U.S. and Canada: 1-800-HOLIDAY

Luxury 17-story downtown hotel with all amenities, half a kilometer from the city center. The hotel is often used as a landmark building when locals are giving directions. It offers 188 rooms, nonsmoking floors, indoor pool, sauna, health club, convention facilities, gymnasium, sauna, business center, restaurants, casino, shops, tour desk, and cable TV.

The Fleur de Lys Hotel ***

Calle 13, Avenidas 2 and 6, San José
Tel: (506) 225-3939 or 224-0505
Fax: (506) 253-6934

Intimate, moderately priced, historic hotel on a quiet street 1 block from the National Museum and the Plaza de la Cultura. This Swiss International hotel is a restored mansion with each of the 19 rooms decorated differently. It also has cable TV, Swiss-Italian restaurant, bar, and parking.

Hotel Europa **

Calle Central, Avenida 5, San José
Tel: (506) 222-1222
Fax: (506) 221-3976
Toll free in the U.S. and Canada: 1-800-223-6764

This smaller European-style hotel has table fans or air-conditioning in the 72 rooms. Facilities include meeting room, restaurant, and small outdoor pool. Rooms on the Calle Central side are very noisy, and pollution comes in through the windows.

Nuevo Hotel Talamanca **

Avenida 2, Calles 8 and 10, San José
Tel: (506) 233-5033
Fax: (506) 233-5420

This small hotel in the center of downtown is quite pleasant, clean, friendly, and newly renovated, but the 52 fan-cooled rooms are small and the neighborhood is dirty, full of traffic, noisy, and busy. There is a restaurant in the hotel, and a great little bar on the top floor that offers bocas (free snacks) every night and features a flamenco guitar player on Friday nights. Stop there for a respite after a day of business.

Gran Hotel Costa Rica *
Apartado 527-1000, San José
Tel: (506) 221-4000
Fax: (506) 221-3501

Located right downtown on Calle 3 between Avenida 2 and Avenida Central, a noisy area. It is located next to a small shopping center and close to the National Theater. This hotel is a historical landmark that badly needs to be renovated. Rooms are cheap. It has 105 rooms, a 24-hour coffee shop, and an outdoor cafe.

San José Suburbs

The suburbs of San José are the place to stay as they are less noisy and are pleasant places to take a stroll. There are always restaurants in these areas.

Camino Real **Recommended*******
Apartado 5895, Escazú, San José
(Boulevard Camino Real)
Tel: (506) 289-7000
Fax: (506) 289-8998
Toll free in the U.S. and Canada: 1-800-722-6466

This large, luxurious, all-amenity resort is located on 3 hectares (7.5 acres) of land in the pleasant suburb of Escazú, about a 10- to 15-minute drive west of San José. The well-decorated, spacious, and clean 261-room hotel offers a business center, health club, 2 pools, tennis court lighted for night play, casino, and nightclub. There is a special club floor with concierge and complimentary breakfasts and cocktails for business travelers.

Cariara Hotel and Country Club **Recommended*******

Apartado 737-1007, Centro Colón, San José
Tel: (506) 239-0022
Fax: (506) 239-2803
Toll free in the U.S. only: 1-800-227-4274

A large, luxurious, all-amenity resort. On Ciudad Cariara, this modern resort and country club is west of San José on the freeway to the airport (10 minutes from the airport and 10 minutes from San José.) It boasts an 18-hole golf course, 10 tennis courts, Olympic-size swimming pool, sauna, Jacuzzi, gymnasium, restaurants, shopping mall, and complimentary shuttle bus to city. There is also a casino and a conference center.

Hotel San José Palacio *****

Urbanizacion el Robledal, La Uruca, San José
Tel: (506) 220-2034
Fax: (506) 220-2036
Toll free in Canada: 1-800-858-0606
Toll free in the U.S.: 1-800-879-8687

This large, modern, 258-room hotel is 5 minutes west of San José on a hill above the freeway to the airport. We found this hotel untidy and decidedly overrated. The hotel has 24 suites, gym, sauna, pool, tennis and racquetball courts, outdoor pool, shops and boutiques, meeting rooms, business center, and casino.

Hotel Bougainvillea **Recommended******
Apartado 69-2120, San José
Tel: (506) 244-1414
Fax: (506) 244-1313

This interesting smaller hotel with the atmosphere of a European country inn is about 15 minutes from downtown, between the Santo Tomas and Santa Rosa areas. The gardens are beautiful and the most extensive in San José. If you want to get away from the rush and pollution of San José, but still have business to do in the city center, this hotel is for you. The 44-room hotel is clean, well decorated, has great views, and offers pool, tennis court, jogging trail, bar and restaurant, and library. Breakfast and a free shuttle bus to San José between 6 a.m. and 11 p.m. are included in the price.

Hotel Herradura ********
Apartado 7-1880, San José
Tel: (506) 239-0033
Fax: (506) 239-2292
Toll free in North America: 1-800-245-8420

A large, modern, Spanish colonial-style hotel approximately 9 km (5.3 mi.) northwest of San José, and close by the Cariara Hotel and Country Club. It is cheaper than the Cariara, but lacks the full resort facilities, although it does have swimming pools, whirlpool, exercise facilities, restaurants, business center, and convention facilities.

Hotel Americano Del Este **Recommended*****
Apartado 303, Los Yoses, San Pedro
(Just north of Autos Subaru)
Tel: (506) 224-2455
Fax: (506) 224-2166

This pleasant, modern, 2-storey hotel has good service, and offers good value. The 29 spacious, fan-cooled rooms in this American-style hotel all have cable TV. Complimentary breakfast is offered to guests in the coffee shop by the pool. The hotel is only 5 minutes from downtown in a pleasant residential area of San Pedro.

Britannia ***
Avenida 11 and Calle 3, Barrio Amon
Tel: (506) 223-6667
Fax: (506) 223-6411

This revamped mansion, adorned by antiques and chandeliers, is a smaller good-value hotel in a historic suburb north of San José. The hotel is clean and the rooms are large but, as in all smaller hotels, amenities are lacking. There are conference rooms for 25 people, a restaurant, and bar.

Hotel Corobici ***

Apartado 2443-1000, San José
(Calle 42, Avenida 5)
Tel: (506) 232-8122
Fax: (506) 231-5834

This large, modern, 275-room tower hotel is just north of Sabana Park in a suburb west of San José. Facilities include pool, health spa, complimentary bus to downtown, restaurant, and bar.

Hotel Gran De Oro ***

Apartado 1157-1007, Centro Colón, San José
Tel: (506) 223-9945 or 255-3322
Fax: (506) 233-2886 or 221-2762

In a large renovated mansion, this feels like an expensive bed and breakfast-style hotel. It is located at 251 Calle 30, on a quiet residential street between Avenidas 2 and 4, in Centro Colón just south of Paseo Colón. It is clean and well decorated, and the service can be quite friendly, but we think it is a bit expensive for what it is. It has 36 rooms, all nonsmoking, a Jacuzzi deck, satellite TV, and a restaurant.

Hotel Ejecutivo Napoleon **

Apartado 8-6340-1000, San José
Tel: (506) 222-2278
Fax: (506) 222-9487

A small, good-value hotel located in a quiet neighborhood just north of the Centro Colón area. It has 27 air-conditioned rooms, cable TV, parking, safety deposit boxes, laundry service, and tour and car rental.

Quality Hotel **

590 Edificio, Centro Colón
Tel: (506) 257-2580
Fax: (506) 257-2582
Toll free in the U.S. and Canada: 1-800-221-2222

This is a typical, good-value Quality Inn. Price and accommodation hover between 2 and 3 stars in this mid-size American chain hotel in the middle of the Centro Colón district. The hotel has 129 rooms on 5 floors and offers in-room coffee, a casino, restaurant, and bar.

Casa Rosa Inn (bed and breakfast)**

Just south of the entrance to La Guaria Country Club, Moravia.
Tel/Fax: (506) 235-9743
Toll free in the U.S. only: 1-800-231-0461

Located in a residential area about 24 km (15 mi.) from downtown, and close to Moravia's souvenir market, this American-owned bed and breakfast features complimentary breakfast with additional meal service available, a conference room, cable TV, secured parking, and use of La Guaria Country Club facilities (Olympic pool, tennis courts, basketball court, restaurant, and bar).

Airport Hotels

San José Hampton Inn **Recommended*****
Alajuela
Tel: (506) 443-0043
Fax: (506) 442-9532
Toll free in Costa Rica: 1-800-426-7866

This clean, modern, airport hotel is near the Juan Santamaría International Airport, and 15 km (9 mi.) from San José. Of the 100 rooms, 75 are non-smoking. Free airport shuttle service, free local calls, and a continental breakfast are included in the room rate. There is an outdoor pool. This is the place to overnight if you have an early morning flight to catch.

Villa Belen *
Tel: (506) 239-0740
Fax: (506) 239-2040

This small Spanish ranch-style courtyard hotel is only 10 minutes from the airport and from San José. It offers a swimming pool and parking.

Liberia

Hotel El Sitio *

Liberia, Guanacaste
In San José, tel: (506) 257-0744
Fax: (506) 257-0745
In Liberia, tel: (506) 666-1211
Fax: (506) 666-2059

Although this is the best hotel in the area, it is nothing to write home about. One block from Inter American Highway, it has 52 rooms, each with a TV, pool, spa, Jacuzzi, restaurant, and convention facility. The rooms are sparsely decorated and simply painted white. This hotel is run down but there is not much choice in Liberia.

Getaways

Guanacaste Province

These beach resorts are reached by driving approximately 4 hours from San José on the Inter American Highway through the Central Valley and the agricultural and cattle lands of Guanacaste province. The road is paved as far as Playas del Coco and Tamarindo on the coast. There is also a newly built airport at Liberia which should have scheduled flights from San José.

Once you have made reservations, your hotel can arrange your ground transportation to and from the hotel. Bring your credit card: the cost of food in resort area restaurants is very high.

Hotel Tamarindo Diria **Recommended*****
Tamarindo, Guanacaste
Tel: (506) 289-8616
Fax: (506) 289-8727

The 70-room hotel is located right on the picturesque beach. All the rooms are pleasant and have air-conditioning, a safety deposit box, and minibar. There is also a pool and restaurant. The Tamarindo area is going through a construction boom and hotels are popping up overnight.

Costa Smeralda ***
Playa Buena, Guanacaste
Tel: (506) 670-0044 or 670-0231 or 670-0032
Fax: (506) 670-0379

This hotel is on the Golfo de Papagayo (Gulf of Papagayo). It is not on the beach, but is pleasant and does have a pool. It has 68 rooms with air-conditioning, satellite TV, minibar, room service, and a very expensive restaurant.

El Ocotal Beach Resort ***
Playas del Coco, Guanacaste
Tel: (506) 670-0321
Fax: (506) 670-0083

This hotel stretches from a cliff down to the beach and features 3 pools, a tennis court, and a restaurant on the premises. The resort is popular with sportfishing enthusiasts. Surfing and fishing trips can be arranged to isolated areas and beaches. At the time of writing, an airport nearby was near completion.

Alajuela Province

Hotel Tilajari **Recommended******

Muelle San Carlos, Alajuela
Tel: (506) 246-1083 or 246-0979
Fax: (506) 246-1462

By far the best hotel in the area, this pleasant, clean, and comfortable establishment was once a country club. It has motel-style rooms with many amenities and comfortable wildlife viewing. All 48 modern, air-conditioned rooms and suites have TV and a private terrace, and the hotel offers a pool, tennis courts, and squash courts.

Situated right by a river, iguanas are often seen on its banks. Sit in the chair on your terrace and watch the grassy area in front of the river come alive with large iguanas. Several tame toucans and a macaw wander freely around the grounds; the macaw often has breakfast on a guest's table. A good base for exploring the area and viewing Arenal or Tabcon Hot Springs.

Tabacon Hot Springs **Recommended Experience**

Tel: (506) 222-1072
Fax: (506) 221-3075

This 5-star hot spring is worth seeing if you are viewing Volcán Arenal. You can hear the volcano boom and see it belch plumes of black smoke, while you sit or swim in one of the many natural mineral water pools. Amenities offered at the hot springs include several hot and cold pools, waterslides, a swim-up bar that also serves snacks, a hot tub, mud masks, massages, and a restaurant. There are also extensive gardens surrounding a boiling hot stream that you can bathe in. Mornings are the quietest time. In the wet season it is often impossible to view Arenal. Across the street is a public hot springs — try this too.

Volcán Arenal **Recommended Experience**

Volcán Arenal is approximately 145 km (90 mi.) from San José, in Alajuela province. Arenal is famous for providing the background volcanic action in the movie *Congo*. It is very active and minor eruptions occur every hour or so. Volcano watching at night is most spectacular as you will see lava flowing down the side of the mountain as well as molten rocks erupting from the top.

The best place to watch the eruptions is not Arenal National Park but Tabacon Hot Springs.

Puntarenas Province

Manuel Antonio National Park, Manuel Antonio village, and the town of Quepos are located on the Pacific Ocean 157 km (97 mi.) from San José, a 3-hour drive from the capital or 20 minutes by air.

Other than the park, there are many better beach destinations than the Manuel Antonio area. Quepos is dirty and there are no decent hotels within walking distance of the beach. Be careful if you go swimming along here as there are many rip tides, and raw sewage is drained right into the water in front of Manuel Antonio.

Manuel Antonio National Park boasts much wildlife and has a few nice beaches, but they can be packed, even in the low season. The third beach, Playa Blanca (Flamingo), is best.

The entrance to the park is a challenge as it involves crossing a creek that can be ankle or chest deep depending on the tide. At high tide a tico is usually there to pull visitors across in a tiny boat.

The park is closed Monday. When it is open, entrance fees will cost you more than the hotel if you bring your family. Expect to pay 2,400 *colones* per person. If you go the day before and buy your tickets, you will pay 1,000 *colones* per person. Locals pay 200 *colones.* Even these high fees don't keep the crowds off the beach or the thieves out. Don't bring anything you would like to keep. There are a few hiking trails within the park as well as toilets and changing rooms.

Villa Caletus **Recommended********

(On the road between Punta Leona and Jaco Beach)
Mailing address: Apartado 12358-1000, San José
Tel: (506) 257-3653
Fax: (506) 222-2059

The hotel brochure lists this establishment's address as "Close to Heaven." One of the most interesting and exclusive properties in Costa Rica,

Villa Caletus is about 100 km (62 mi.) from San José on the road to the Pacific beach resorts.

This hilltop 5-star hotel has a magnificent view of the Pacific and a tropical mountain resort setting. Everything about this 8-room, 15-bungalow hotel is unique. The grounds and buildings are magnificently done. Facilities include a bar, restaurant, pool, and a Roman-style amphitheater where small concerts are presented for the enjoyment of hotel guests in green season. In August there is an international festival of music with concert packages available. This hotel is worth a visit if only for lunch and a look around.

El Parador Hotel and Beach Club **Recommended******
Quepos, Puntarenas
Tel: (506) 777-1414
Fax: (506) 777-1437

This is an unusual and truly grand hotel with a great view and magnificent furnishings. It is decorated in a Spanish Mediterranean style, which the designers went to great lengths to perfect. The hotel houses many artifacts and 50 antique European paintings. It is a unique place and worth a visit, if only for lunch. If you plan to stay, there are 55 rooms or suites, a library, wine cellar, tennis court, pool, and Jacuzzi. Accommodation is in villas scattered around the main building. This hotel is quite expensive during the high season.

Tulemar Bungalows ****

On the road between Manuel Antonio and Quepos
Tel: (506) 777-0580
Fax: (506) 777-1579

These relatively expensive bungalows are pleasant, large, and clean. Each has a kitchenette, air-conditioning, phone, TV, VCR, and safe. There is a pool and an agreeable beachfront. Unfortunately, the bungalows are located on top of a large hill, so it is necessary to drive down to the hotel's beach.

Rancho Casa Grande ***

Quepos, Puntarenas
Tel: (506) 777-0330
Fax: (506) 777-1575

Although this hotel is expensive for the area, and is about 10 minutes away from Manuel Antonio beach, it is worth the stay. The bungalows are well decorated and clean. There is a pool and spa. But what makes this hotel special is the jungle trails that are part of the grounds. The trails, through both primary- and secondary-growth jungle, will take you up to 3 hours to complete and are constantly being expanded. The jungle and the animal life it contains are as good as any you'll find in a park. Self-guide books are available free of charge, and the owner is often willing to guide people through.

Cartago Province

Volcán Irazú — Recommended Experience

Irazú is a 3-hour round trip from San José and is usually done as a daytrip. The volcano isn't very active, but will occasionally produce a gas bubble in the lake in the volcanic crater. The smell of sulfur can be quite strong. The view itself is spectacular and on a clear day you can see both oceans, as Irazu is the highest point in Costa Rica. Temperatures average 11°C (52°F), so a warm coat wouldn't be amiss. It is important to remember to take it easy up on the summit; the slightest bit of exercise will leave most gasping for air in the thin atmosphere. However, most tourists stay for such a short time that altitude sickness never becomes a problem.

Limón Province

Las Palmas Resort Hotel ***

Punta Uva, Limón
Tel: (506) 255-3939
Fax: (506) 255-3737

An hour's drive south of Limón, close to the Gandoca-Manzanillo Wildlife Reserve, this beach resort on the Caribbean has a 26-foot cruiser available for rent. Diving, hiking, and horseback riding can be arranged. Hotel facilities include restaurant, pool, beach bar, and ocean view rooms.

Miraflores Lodge **
Tel: (506) 233-2822
Fax: (506) 233-2822

Located south of Limón near Puerto Viejo, Miraflores is about a 3½ hour drive from San José. This pleasant hotel is close to the beach and is a working flower farm. Since it is quite close to the Panamanian border, guests can visit Panama's remote northern region as well as several nearby Indian villages. The staff at Miraflores Lodge sponsor sustainable agriculture and ecological projects; one involves the local Keküldi clan which raises iguanas for release in the forest.

Casa Río Blanco Country Inn (bed and breakfast)*
Apartado 241-7210, Guapiles, Limón
Tel: (506) 382-0957
Fax: (506) 710-6161

This bed and breakfast hotel is located on the way to Limón and the Caribbean, close to Don Perry's Rainforest Tram. (This tram is worth visiting. It allows you to view the rainforest canopy from above, where you see many birds and animals that are invisible if you are looking up from the ground.) The hotel has a natural swimming hole and a natural whitewater Jacuzzi. Breakfast is included in your room rate, as is 1 hour with a naturalist guide. Optional hikes range from 3 to 8 hours. This hotel is within an hour's drive of San José. Single rooms, from US $35, are basic.

Hotel Ilan Ilan *

Tortuguero
Tel: (506) 255-2031
Fax: (506) 255-1946

This lodge offers small and Spartan rooms with concrete floors and cots. They are fitted with slow rotating fans, no hot water, unbearable mosquitoes, and oppressive heat. There is no place to swim or cool off, in or out of your room. Expect to put up with a nowhere hotel in a fascinating place.

The only amenity this lodge has is its location on the canals and the remarkable jungle experience of getting there; if you lust for a jungle adventure, this or any of the other nearby lodges are the places to go.

Canal de Tortuguero Recommended Experience

The Canal de Tortuguero is an area of rivers, lagoons, and estuaries that run for 160 km (100 mi.) through Costa Rica's northern coastal region in Limón Province. Tortuguero village is nestled on the southern edge of the Barra del Colorado National Park, but the Spartan tour hotels that provide the only sleeping and eating base for your adventure are located out of the village and on the canal. The heat is oppressive and no hotels have pools, as the area floods often. The ocean and rivers are infested with crocodiles and sharks, so swimming is impossible.

The attraction is nature as it was meant to be: sloths, howler monkeys, caimans, crocodiles, rich and varied jungle vegetation, and a variety of birds are easily seen on the canals. Turtle spawning season (July/August) is the best time to visit.

Tortuguero isn't very accessible, and it is hard to get there without a tour or some sort of package. There is an air strip for those with little time and lots of money. Going by boat is a lot more fun, and can be the best part of the experience.

The tour itinerary is 4 hours by bus and another 4 by boat along wildlife-rich rivers and canals. The boat ride involves jungle exploration and many animal sightings. During turtle spawning season you will be taken by a guide to view the turtles laying eggs. This is a once-in-a-lifetime experience. If you go, make sure you pack light but carry everything you need, especially insect repellent, as there are no stores around the hotel. Basic meals are included in the tour package.

Fishing Adventures

Río Colorado Lodge **

Barra del Colorado
Tel: (506) 232-8610
Toll free in the United States: 1-800-243-9777

Río Colorado offers fishing packages for the diehard fisher/business traveler in one of the most unspoiled places in the world. The rates are expensive, but airfare from San José is included. You are flown in to give you maximum time on the water.

Don't expect anything fancy, just great fishing and basic comforts. Meals are included.

Whitewater Rafting

Costa Rica offers many opportunities for whitewater rafting due to its mountainous terrain and abundance of rivers. There are as many tour companies as rivers. Tours run from different areas around the country. Any hotel should be able to book you on a trip with a company that leaves from the area you are in. There are also nonprofit organizations that run tours and donate the money to various worthy causes. These are of the same quality as the other organizations except the profit doesn't go into someone's pocket. If you go, check to see if the company is fully licensed with professional and English-speaking guides.

Dos Ríos Whitewater Rafting
Tel: (506) 556-7834 or 556-1111

This is a Texas-based company that runs both paddle and non paddle trips, depending on whether you want to join in or have both hands clutching your camera.

Save the Rain Forests Expeditions and School
Quepos, Puntarenas
Tel: (506) 777-1495 or 777-1495

This outfit arranges rafting trips on the Savegre, Naranjo, and Nunawachi mountain rivers on the

Pacific coast. Instead of paying to go on these trips, you make a set tax-deductible donation. Money goes toward environmental education, sustainable agricultural projects, and voluntary wildlife and forestry inspectors program, to name a few. Guides are bilingual and have Red Cross first-aid certification. Though the office is in Puntarenas, you can book your place on a trip in tour offices around Costa Rica.

Cruise Getaways

Cruising is the ultimate way to get a quick feel for a place or to have a stress-free vacation without any hassles. There are no suitcases to pack, unpack, and carry; food is plentiful and usually good or excellent. The biggest decision to make on a cruise is where to have lunch or what to wear for dinner.

Cunard Line **Recommended*******

Toll-free reservations in the U.S. and Canada:
1-800-221-4770

If you prefer a medium-size, ultra-deluxe ship that you share with 700 to 800 passengers, the *Royal Viking Sun* and *Vistafjord* have sailings that transit the Panama Canal and stop in Costa Rica. *Vistafjord* holds an exclusive ultra-deluxe rating from the World Ocean and Cruise Liner Society. All amenities are offered (except stern platform for water sports directly off the ship). The *Royal Viking* is rated in *Condé Nast Traveler* magazine's top 10 list for recreation and entertainment on larger ships.

Sea Goddess 1 **Recommended*****

Toll-free reservations in the U.S. and Canada: 1-800-528-6273

Very expensive, but you are getting all the amenities. The small, elegant *Sea Goddess 1* offers a range of 14-day cruises through the Panama Canal with stops in Costa Rica during January and February. A limit of only 116 pampered guests, with a cruise staff of 89, means this feels like being on your own private yacht. The *Sea Goddess 1* offers 58 large outside suites, complimentary liquor, complimentary in-suite bar and fridge, 24-hour in-suite meal and beverage service, TV, VCR, stereo, Michelin-rated dining salon, complimentary in-pool cocktail parties with caviar and champagne, Golden Door Spa at Sea, a stern platform for water sports directly from the ship, and no tipping. Suits those who prefer intimate, exclusive, and decadent.

Princess Cruises **Recommended****

Toll free in the U.S. and Canada: 1-800-568-3262

If you want to travel on a larger ship with more passengers, Princess Cruises of *Love Boat* fame offer Panama Canal cruises that stop briefly in Costa Rica from late September through April. These are expensive 12- to 22-day cruises originating out of Ft. Lauderdale. All ships are large luxury ships carrying from 1,200 to 1,900 passengers, offering all the usual cruise ship amenities (except stern platform for water sports directly off the ship).

Temptress Explorer **Ecoadventure*****

Toll free in the U.S. and Canada: 1-800-336-8423

Temptress Voyages offers 3- and 6-night cruises out of and around Costa Rica on the *Temptress Explorer*. This 50-cabin ship, built in Seattle and launched in late 1995, was especially designed with a shallow draft to reach shallow rivers and bays. The *Temptress Explorer* visits Curú Biological Reserve, Corcovado National Park, Golfo Dulce Forest Reserve, and the Golfito National Wildlife Refuge.

At press time we learned that the *Temptress* now has a 3- and 7-day itinerary out of Belize city that includes manatee (sea cow) viewing and a visit to a Mayan ceremonial center that is under excavation.

Water sports directly from the ship.

Other books in the *Kick Start* Series:

Hong Kong, Macau, and the Pearl River Delta
ISBN 1-55180-043-8
$9.95 168 pp.

Indonesia
ISBN 0-88908-844-6
$9.95 160 pp.

Malaysia
ISBN 0-88908-845-4
$9.95 160 pp.

Vietnam
ISBN 0-88908-843-8
$9.95 160 pp.

If you would like to receive a free catalogue of all Self-Counsel titles, please write to the appropriate address below:

Self-Counsel Press
1481 Charlotte Road
North Vancouver, B.C.
V7J 1H1

Self-Counsel Press
1704 N. State Street
Bellingham, WA 98225